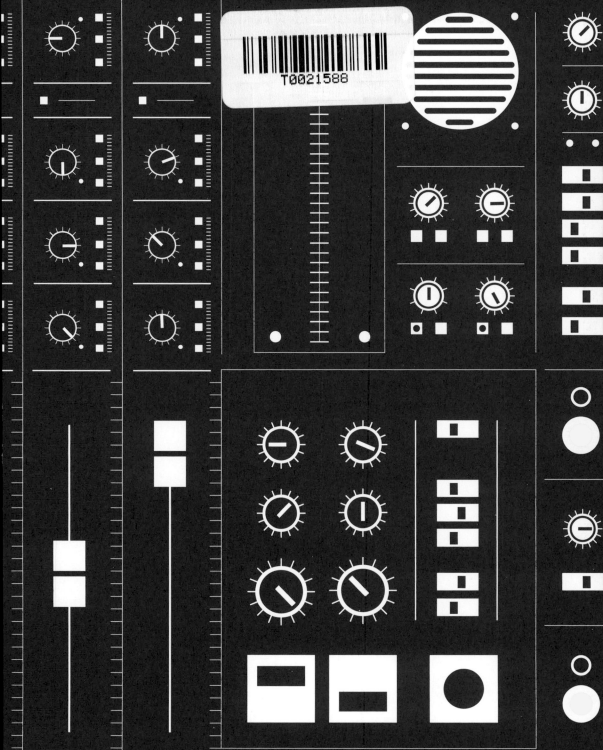

Post-Punk & New Wave.

STEVE WIDE
PRESENTS

A
field
guide
to

Post
Punk
& New
Wave.

Smith
Street
Books

Contents.

What I took into Depeche (Mode) was that punk ethic, that you don't have to be accomplished to be a musician. If you've got ideas, you can do this.

DAVE GAHAN, DEPECHE MODE, SPIN, NOVEMBER 2007

... you can never underestimate the impact of Kraftwerk. *Trans-Europe Express* had the same impact on the synth poppers that 'Anarchy In The UK' had on people who wanted to be punk rockers.

SIMON REYNOLDS, SYNTH BRITANNIA, 2009

... they (punks) were the older generation that needed taking down a peg or two. Looking back on it now those punk rock princes, a few of them turned into frogs ... and thirty years later they just look like fat, bloated drunkards ... I'm very proud of my generation ... (they) stood for ... anti-sexism ... there weren't a lot of girls in punk rock (bands), but there were a lot of girls in the indie scene ... Gillian Gilbert from New Order was a real pioneer ...

JOHNNY MARR, FAR & WIDE
(WITH STEVE WIDE), 2014

Along with Patti Smith and Siouxsie Sioux, I was changing the way women in bands were perceived. It was a whole new era and we were like warriors. I wasn't going to be told by my record company how to look.

DEBBIE HARRY,
MAIL ON SUNDAY, 2014

When punk came along, I found my generation's music. I grew up listening to the Beatles and the Rolling Stones and Pink Floyd, 'cause that was what got played in the house. But when I first saw the Stranglers, I thought, "This is it." And I saw the Buzzcocks the following week, and I thought, "This is definitely it."

ROBERT SMITH, THE CURE,
JULY 2004

The bleak & the beautiful.

Punk's mainstream popularity crashed and burned within the space of two years, but it set in motion a pop pinwheel that spins to this very day. After punk a host of bands who hadn't been to music school – or even a single music lesson – appeared. But what they lacked in music degrees they more than made up for in burning ambition, natural aptitude, raging discontent and a desperate need for a creative outlet. In many ways John Lydon – aka Johnny Rotten, leader of the Sex Pistols, who had brought punk into the collective consciousness of the UK and beyond – was also the impetus for post-punk, seeing the writing on the filthy bathroom wall and calling time out on the movement that had propelled him to infamy. His follow up to the Sex Pistols, Public Image Ltd, or PiL, was a gloom-tinged, spiky hard centre with soft edges that defined the burgeoning post-punk and new wave movements. Booming drums, cavernous vocals, barely concealed spite … it was punk without the rock, and music without a guidebook and few definable historical references. Post-punk was the perfect name, because it had needed punk in order to happen. Once it was past that, however, punk was no longer a reference point.

Bands sprung up overnight. Intense, existential, taciturn, arrogant, political and defensive, they wore Dr. Martens boots, overcoats and dark colours, had lank hair, played keyboards that clashed with guitars, purveyed two-chord drones, vitriol with a message, obscurity with the power to move you. Music was abrasive and distancing, painful and powerful, but most of all it was suddenly limitless, floating in a space teeming with possibilities, a living entity that was part liberated and energised, part anxious and insecure. Even the band names reflected a new attitude: Joy Division, The Cure, Devo, Wire, Gang of Four, Talking Heads.

New wave was a different matter entirely. The new wavers were Serious Young Things, for sure, but with a fashion sense and a university degree. They wore thin ties, pointy shoes, shoulder pads and pleated pants. Their hair was spiky and high. With synthesisers becoming more affordable and the guitar seemingly reaching its limits as an instrument in the pop world, the time was right for a new sound. Instruments that 'played themselves' were de rigueur, though the synth bands insisted it took a science degree to read the manual to work out how to use them. Poseurs in tight pants stood rigidly behind their synths, perhaps making the occasional leg movement or throwing a sideways glance. This wasn't the rock-god guitar stance or drum solo – this was the serious business of pop music. Band names reflected the philosophy – Orchestral Manoeuvres in the Dark, Simple Minds, Tubeway Army, Depeche Mode, The Human League. Experimental, catchy, melodic, atmospheric, moody and gloomy, new wave, with its keyboards and programming, took over the charts worldwide. Guitars weren't entirely excluded – new wave was a style that encompassed punchy, chord-driven, witty, lyrical and fast-paced pop music that relied on the short sharp shock of punk but turned it into verse-chorus-verse chart bait. Purveyors of this sound included Elvis Costello & the Attractions, XTC and Blondie.

Together, post-punk and new wave altered music forever, and despite a slicker-than-slick '80s sheen washing out the overly sincere intentions of the early adopters, the legacy of that era has been as far-reaching as that of punk, the genre that spawned it.

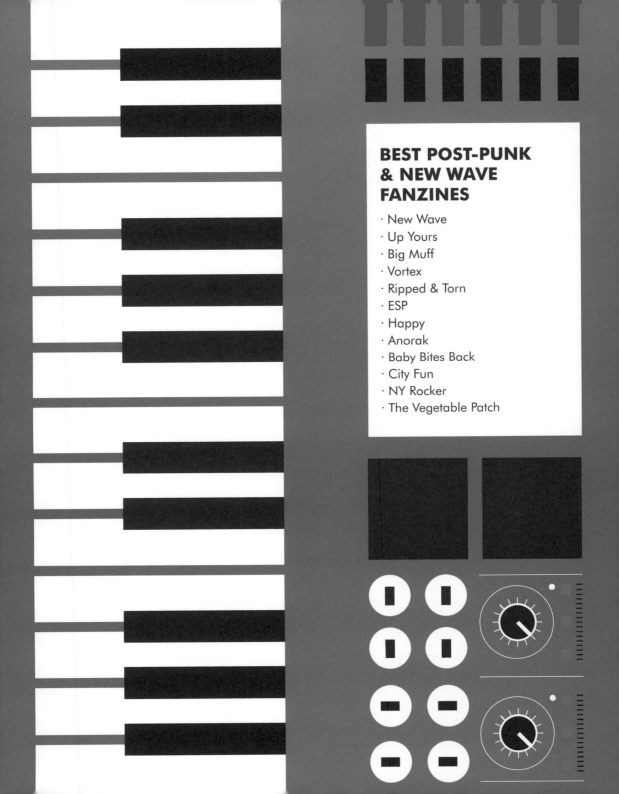

BEST POST-PUNK & NEW WAVE FANZINES

· New Wave
· Up Yours
· Big Muff
· Vortex
· Ripped & Torn
· ESP
· Happy
· Anorak
· Baby Bites Back
· City Fun
· NY Rocker
· The Vegetable Patch

When & why.

As the '70s drew to a close, punk started to sound too much like rock music. Something new was happening. Punk had opened the doors, creating a DIY ethic and a defiant attitude that reached out across the world. All of a sudden, anyone who wanted to be in a band was willing to give it a shot. What mattered was passion, invention and being cutting-edge – the first to play or program a synth in a particular way, the one with the darkest lyrics or most ethereal sound, the first to meld certain instruments or dress or do their hair in a new and interesting way. Things were changing. Economies were picking up. The unemployed could get financial assistance, which they often used to fund their creativity. Rents were relatively cheap. In the UK, education became more affordable under the new Conservative government, especially if you were studying to get into a trade. Or, if you were particularly talented, you could get a scholarship. Along with that came Margaret Thatcher, whose reforms to the welfare state and industry had varying degrees of success, giving bands much that they could be angry about and rail against. There was a boom in discontented university bands with a penchant for the experimental and a flair for the dramatic. Lyrics became intensely political or deeply philosophical.

A strange dichotomy existed between the UK and the USA. (Australia took in elements of both, while Europe tracked an eccentric path of its own.) While post-punk exploded in the UK, in the USA it remained mostly underground, with the bands the darlings of the independent and alternative charts. New wave straddled both worlds. In the USA, it manifested in bands born of the art rock and college scenes that became hugely successful, like Blondie, Talking Heads, Devo and The B-52s. The Cars' first LP is said to have sold one million copies in a year and spent 139 weeks on the Billboard charts.

Post-punk and new wave signalled that rock was over. Standard guitar chord structures and sounds were passé. Technology was booming and synthesisers, other electronic instruments and recording became cheaper, meaning that regular people with an interest in music could get their hands on the latest gadgets and use them to create new forms of music. Moods, soundscapes and atmosphere were blended with impressive, arty visuals. For that short period between 1978 and 1984, music would be restless, experimental, exploratory and revolutionary.

Evolution.

Post-punk was just that – it came after punk – and would be forever linked to punk, despite having many stark differences. New wave was an offshoot of post-punk, so also owes an allegiance to punk, despite being in many ways something a lot of punks would despise. But it was all about the freedom, experimentation and expression – punk had shown that the everyday person could 'live the dream' and make their own record. Some were content to do only that – have a one-off flourish that might be consigned to the bargain bin, possibly to live another day and be proclaimed an influential masterpiece, or be forever lost. Others may have intended to make that one statement and then move on, but found that a whole generation of similarly displaced people connected with the music, and as time went on had continued success – even a career.

Punk may have been a catalyst for the evolution of post-punk and new wave throughout the late '70s and early '80s, but there were other reference points, too. David Bowie's so-called Berlin trilogy – *Heroes* (1977), *Lodger* (1979) and in particular, *Low* (1977), on which Brian Eno was a musical collaborator and Tony Visconti producer – predicted how music would develop. Side one of *Low* features short, direct, bleak, emotive tunes. Punchy and melodic, they are also imbued with a triumphant bravado, despite being insular in intent. Side two favours glorious synth washes, anthemic in their own way, which inspired the loftier elements of new wave and New Romantic music.

Eno had tracked the sound in his albums *Here Come The Warm Jets* (1973), *Taking Tiger Mountain (By Strategy)* (1974) and *Another Green World* (1975). Songs like 'Third Uncle' sounded punk and post-punk well before both genres existed. Most of *Another Green World* is new wave pop magic – seven years before the fact. For good measure Eno threw in 'Becalmed', one of the best instrumentals ever made with a synthesiser, and in doing so predicted ambient as well as new wave in a single four-minute flourish.

Ultravox, which had formed as Tiger Lily in London in 1973/74 and were renamed Ultravox in 1976, blended punk, awkward sexuality and sinister collage with punchy guitars, synthesiser hook lines and robotic disconnection under original leader John Foxx. The Pop Group, formed in Bristol in 1977, released two records – 1979's *Y* and 1980's *For How Much Longer Do We Tolerate Mass Murder?* – characterised by angst-ridden, strident vocals and repetitious, propulsive guitar lines that both post-punk and later bands used as their sound template. Wire made edgy, abrupt pop with captivating lyrics while eschewing the standard verse-chorus-verse structure of pop. Gang of Four wove their political sensibilities into their angular, skittish punk funk. The Residents, Pere Ubu, James Chance & The Contortions … so many bands were willing to push the envelope and in doing so sculpted a brave new musical world.

Germany's Kraftwerk saw the future, 'krafting' cinematic soundscapes from electronic impulse and diode. Their ear for a melody would ensure that mechanical repetition could still strike a chord with the everyday listener – as Orchestral Manoeuvres in the Dark once put it, 'people like a tune they can hum in the bath', and Kraftwerk knew how to do just that. 'The Model', 'Neon Lights' and 'Pocket Calculator', while possessing a Teutonic steeliness, were somehow still warm. Kraftwerk were like cyborgs desperate to show that they were human, and their approach to music would be highly influential. Punk, Eno, Bowie, Kraftwerk, glam rock – it all melded into a sound that both captured and transcended the times, influencing generations. Music for the brain and the heart, post-punk and new wave was by and for the futurists, the sonic explorers, the social innovators. Bedroom-dwelling music fans found heroes in Morrissey, Robert Smith, Ian Curtis, Gary Numan and others. This was music by misfits, for misfits.

1963
Electronic music composer Delia Derbyshire reworks Ron Grainer's *Doctor Who* theme.

1964
Robert Moog debuts the Moog synthesiser.

1973
Brian Eno, *Here Come The Warm Jets* and *Taking Tiger Mountain*; The Residents, *Meet The Residents*; Kraftwerk, 'Autobahn'.

Post-Punk & New Wave timeline.

1978
Magazine, 'Shot By Both Sides'; The Normal, 'Warm Leatherette'; Joy Division, *An Ideal For Living* EP; The Human League, 'Being Boiled'; Siouxsie and the Banshees, 'Hong Kong Garden'; Devo, *Q: Are We Not Men? A: We Are Devo!*;

Cabaret Voltaire, *Extended Play* EP; Siouxsie and the Banshees, *The Scream*; The Cure, 'Killing an Arab'; Public Image Ltd, *Public Image First Issue*. Rough Trade Records and Factory Records established.

1980 cont'd
→ The Human League, *Travelogue*; The Birthday Party, *The Birthday Party*; Magazine, *The Correct Use of Soap*; Joy Division, 'Love Will Tear Us Apart', *Closer*; Bow Wow Wow,

'C 30, C 60, C 90 Go'; Devo, 'Whip It'; Simple Minds, *Empires and Dance*; Talking Heads, *Remain in Light*; Visage, 'Fade to Grey'; Japan, *Gentlemen Take Polaroids*; Ian Curtis commits suicide.

1981
New Order, *Movement*; David Byrne and Brian Eno, *My Life in the Bush of Ghosts*; Duran Duran, 'Planet Earth'; The Birthday Party, *Prayers on Fire*; PiL, *The Flowers of Romance*; The Human League, *Dare*; The Cure, *Faith*; Depeche Mode, 'New Life', 'Just Can't

Get Enough'; Heaven 17, *Penthouse and Pavement*; Simple Minds, *Sons and Fascination*; Laurie Anderson, 'O Superman'; Orchestral Manoeuvres in the Dark, *Architecture & Morality*; Kraftwerk, 'The Model'.

1975

Kim Ryrie and Peter Vogel launch the Fairlight company. Brian Eno, *Another Green World*; Pere Ubu, '30 Seconds Over Tokyo'.

1977

Elvis Costello performs 'Radio Radio' on *Saturday Night Live*. Sex Pistols, *Never Mind The Bollocks*; Wire, *Pink Flag*; Brian Eno, *Before and After Science*; David Bowie, *Low*; Buzzcocks, *Spiral Scratch EP*; Iggy Pop, *The Idiot*; Devo, 'Mongoloid'; Kraftwerk, *Trans-Europe Express*; Talking Heads, *Talking Heads: 77*; Throbbing Gristle, *The Second Annual Report of Throbbing Gristle*.

1979

Joy Division perform 'Transmission' and 'She's Lost Control' on the BBC's *Something Else*; Tubeway Army perform 'Are "Friends" Electric?' on *Top of the Pops*. Joy Division, *Unknown Pleasures*; Gang of Four, *Entertainment!*; The Pop Group, *Y*; The Fall, *Live at the Witch Trials*; Public Image Ltd, 'Death Disco'; Gary Numan, 'Cars'; The Slits, *Cut*; Bauhaus, 'Bela Lugosi's Dead'; Wire, *154*; The Human League, *Reproduction*; Buggles, 'Video Killed the Radio Star'; PiL, *Metal Box*. The Fairlight CMI synthesiser and sampler is released.

1980

The Cure, *Seventeen Seconds*; The Pop Group, *For How Much Longer Do We Tolerate Mass Murder?*; Joy Division, 'Atmosphere'; John Foxx, *Metamatic*; The Jam, 'Going Underground', →

1982

MIDI, electronic synchronisation (joining synthesiser and drum machine) become available to the public. Japan, 'Ghosts'; The Cure, *Pornography*; New Order, 'Temptation'; ABC, *The Lexicon of Love*; Cocteau Twins, *Garlands*.

1983

The Smiths perform 'This Charming Man' on *Top of the Pops*. OMD, *Dazzle Ships*; Echo & the Bunnymen, *Porcupine*; The Birthday Party, *The Bad Seed EP*; New Order, 'Blue Monday', Heaven 17, 'Temptation'; PiL, 'This Is Not a Love Song'; The Sisters of Mercy, 'Temple of Love'.

1984

The Smiths, *The Smiths*; Propaganda, 'The Nine Lives of Dr. Mabuse'; Echo & the Bunnymen, *Ocean Rain*; Bronski Beat, 'Smalltown Boy'; Depeche Mode, 'People Are People'.

Post-Punk & New Wave family trees.

Legend:
- Key artists
- Spinoffs
- Spinoff spinoffs
- World event
- Music genre
- Technology
- Tech artists

Ian McCulloch

Bow Wow Wow

Adam and the Ants

Echo & the Bunnymen

Revenge

New Order

Adam Ant

The Monochrome Set

Modest Mouse

Electrafixion

Joy Division

The Glove

The Other Two

The The

Johnny Marr

The Cribs

Electronic

Siouxsie and the Banshees

Electronic

The Smiths

Morrissey

Psychedelic Furs

Love Spit Love

The Creatures

Badly Drawn Boy

Andy Rourke

Magazine

Public Image Ltd.

Sex Pistols

Malcolm McLaren

Sharp

The Style Council

Buzzcocks

Wire

Dome

Bow Wow Wow

The Jam

Paul Weller

Howard Devoto

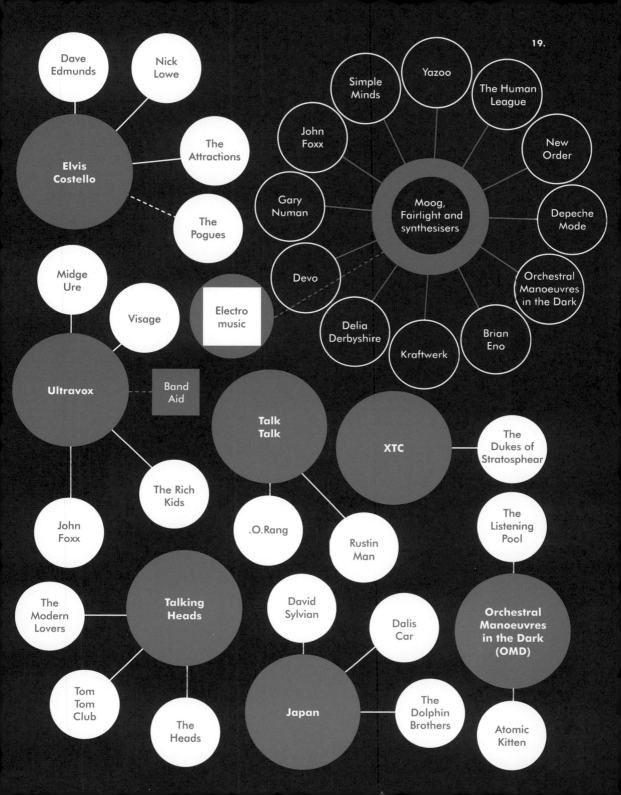

Post-Punk & New Wave:

The defining albums.

JOY DIVISION
Unknown Pleasures

Released: June 1979

Label: Factory

Producer: Martin Hannett

Listen: 'Disorder', 'She's Lost Control', 'Shadowplay', 'New Dawn Fades'

Chart placing: Didn't chart on initial release (UK chart #5, 40th anniversary reissue)

Trivia: Producer Hannett used effects units, but also relied on natural sounds, tape loops of smashing bottles, guitars played backwards, and the sound of Strawberry Studios' lift, the basement toilet and even someone eating potato chips.

Also listen: *Closer*

✖ JOY DIVISION had recently changed their name from Warsaw and released an EP, *An Ideal for Living*. In 1978, as Warsaw, they had recorded an LP, featuring several tracks that would appear on *Unknown Pleasures*. Joy Division's debut LP didn't chart on initial release, yet it remains the defining album of post-punk. *Unknown Pleasures* is dark, unrelenting, unrepentant and exhilarating, with a claustrophobic, desperate sadness and doomed romanticism woven around sparse guitar lines and echoing drums. Peter Saville designed the iconic sleeve, a waveform data representation of a radio pulsar, the beam from a visible neutron star. Martin Hannett's production on the album was experimental and revolutionary. Considering punk rock recording techniques conservative, Hannett set about using instruments and sounds that would create atmosphere and tension and highlight silence and space. For 'Insight', he recorded Ian Curtis' voice down a telephone line. Despite not charting on initial release, *Unknown Pleasures* is widely regarded as one of the greatest albums recorded and a major influence on Goth, alternative, indie, industrial and even dance music.

THE CURE
Seventeen Seconds

Released: 22 April 1980
Label: Fiction
Producers: Mike Hedges, Robert Smith
Listen: 'A Forest', Play For Today',
'M', 'In Your House'
Chart placing: UK chart #20

Trivia: The drums on the album sound robotic and programmed, but they are in fact the sound of drummer Lol Tolhurst playing along to the beat of a strobe light.

Also listen: *Faith,
Pornography, Disintegration*

✖ THE CURE'S first LP, *Three Imaginary Boys*, and subsequent US release, *Boys Don't Cry*, couldn't have prepared anyone for the dark, minimal direction that the band would go in for their next three albums. The single 'Boys Don't Cry' was jaunty and upbeat, and a similarly melodic thread ran through much of their other early material. However, *Seventeen Seconds* would start The Cure on a path that would get darker and darker. It's a sparse, atmospheric record tinged with folk horror, references to Gothic novels and noir poetry. Lead single 'A Forest' is a dark tale of a phantom girl who would run into the forest and disappear. 'A Forest' was a top 40 hit in the UK and successful over the world, and remains one of the Cure's classic singles. 'Play for Today' is also a standout among the broody instrumentals and nihilistic, morose tunes like 'M' and 'In Your House'. The title track is truly bleak, but perfectly rounds off an album that stood apart from its contemporaries and set the stage for the Gothic rock and indie introspection that would dominate the underground charts through the '80s.

ORCHESTRAL MANOEUVRES IN THE DARK
Architecture & Morality

Released: 6 November 1981
Label: Dindisc
Producers: OMD, Mike Howlett, Richard Manwaring
Listen: 'Joan of Arc (Maid of Orleans)' aka 'Maid of Orleans (The Waltz Joan of Arc)', 'Souvenir', 'Joan of Arc', 'She's Leaving', 'Sealand'
Chart placing: UK chart #3 (#1 Holland)

Trivia: Stirring album track 'She's Leaving' is widely considered the OMD single that never was. The band said that the record company wanted to release it as a fourth single, but at the time OMD thought that would be milking the album.

Also listen: *Organisation, Dazzle Ships*

✖ AFTER A PUNKY, pacy debut and a gloomy, Joy Division–inspired second LP (*Organisation*, featuring classic single 'Enola Gay'), OMD reset themselves and produced, in *Architecture & Morality*, a seminal synth-pop album that would become a template for electronic music. Boasting three top 10 singles, including two OMD staples, 'Souvenir' and 'Joan of Arc (Maid of Orleans)', *Architecture & Morality* pulses with invention, innovation and surprise without ever becoming pretentious. Recognising that electronic music didn't have to be robotic, OMD layered choral sounds over sparse drums and built up a weightier sound palette, enhancing it with atmospherics and stories. The album kicks off with an abrasive, thrashy guitar strum accented by Andy McCluskey's desperate, imploring vocal and overlaid with a strident keyboard line, hoodwinking the listener into thinking that the album will be a dark journey into the psyche of a madman. However, your ears are then gently massaged by some of electronic pop's most emotive melodies and you fall hook, line and coda. 'She's Leaving', 'Souvenir' and the 'Joan of Arc' twins (McCluskey had originally wanted to release them both under the same title to confuse listeners) are magical moments where the synthesiser creates truly dulcet, moving music.

WIRE
Pink Flag

Released: November 1977
Label: Harvest
Producer: Mike Thorne
Listen: 'Three Girl Rhumba',
'Mannequin'
Chart placing: Didn't chart

Trivia: The first pressing of *Pink Flag* featured 21 songs in a 36 minute running time.

Also listen: *Chairs Missing, 154*

✖ WITH *PINK FLAG*, Wire rewrote the rule book on music, albums and attitude. Existing concurrently with punk rock, they picked up on the DIY ethos, rebelliousness and defiant individualism, yet eschewed the nihilism and anger. Like punk rock, *Pink Flag* was crude and unstudied, but unlike punk it was organic and fertile, creating a rich bed from which new bands and sounds would spring up in abundance. Perversely, it was also aloof and exclusive, but this clearly didn't deter would-be musicians, given the many bands that materialised in Wire's wake. Influencing scenes as diverse as post-punk, new wave, hardcore, alternative and even Britpop, *Pink Flag* was the sound of a band with something new and original to say. The album contained 21 tracks, almost unheard-of for a single album at the time. The songs were short, furious, clipped and concise. The shortest track, 'Field Day for the Sundays', comes in at 28 seconds. Replete with distorted noise, desperation, stop-start dynamics, and often surprising rhythms and arrangements, *Pink Flag* sees Wire questioning everything. Progressive rock it wasn't, but progressive it most certainly was.

GANG OF FOUR
Entertainment!

Released: 25 September 1979

Label: EMI

Producers: Andy Gill, Jon King, Rob Warr

Listen: 'Love Like Anthrax', 'At Home He's a Tourist', 'Natural's Not In It', 'Damaged Goods', 'Guns Before Butter'

Chart placing: UK chart #45

Trivia: The NME placed *Entertainment!* at number five on its 1979 Albums of the Year list.

Also listen: *Solid Gold, Songs of the Free*

✖ **LIKE WIRE**, Gang of Four tapped into the energy and vitriol of punk but refused to be bound by punk's rigid three-chord guitar structures. Instead, Gang of Four used their debut album, *Entertainment!*, to fuse punk with dub, reggae, dance music and funk. Not that it sounded like any of those things. The angular beats and dissonant delivery saw Gang of Four slip deftly through one of the many doors opened by punk to create a challenging and inventive new sound that would become a jumping-off point for post-punk and influence artists as disparate as Kurt Cobain, Michael Hutchence of INXS and Flea from the Red Hot Chili Peppers. Themes included consumerism, politics, Northern Ireland and challenges to accepted theories on society, sex and love. Fractured and defiant, with minimal melodies, few discernable choruses and persistently ranting, mechanical vocals, *Entertainment!* doesn't sound like a candidate for chart success, but it managed to breach the UK top 50.

THE SMITHS
The Smiths

Released: 24 February 1984
Label: Rough Trade
Producer: John Porter
Listen: 'This Charming Man',
'Still Ill', 'Hand in Glove',
'What Difference Does It Make?'
Chart placing: UK chart #2

Trivia: The cover image is of Joe Dallesandro, one of Andy Warhol's Factory gang. The still is taken from Warhol's film *Flesh*. Morrissey's practice of featuring his heroes on record sleeves would continue throughout The Smiths' career.

Also listen: *Meat is Murder, The Queen is Dead, Strangeways, Here We Come*

✖ BY THE TIME THE SMITHS' DEBUT came out the band had already been touring relentlessly and had garnered a healthy following. An instant hit on release, staying in the charts for an impressive 33 weeks, the album was unlike anything else around at the time. The public taste was for upbeat, synth-driven pop with shiny production and lyrics about love and success. The Smiths steamrolled through all of that with chiming, jubilant guitar lines offset by Morrissey's observational, stark, often tongue-in-cheek lyrics. With its themes of personal inadequacy, outsiderdom and Manchester's grubbier side, peppered with literary and cinematic references, the album was a manifesto for bedroom rebels all over the UK and, subsequently, the world. Stand-out single 'This Charming Man', which The Smiths performed on *Top of the Pops*, would become one of the band's most recognisable tunes. 'Suffer Little Children' bravely and poignantly addressed Manchester's grim Moors Murders, while 'Pretty Girls Make Graves' and 'Miserable Lie' candidly discuss Morrissey's inadequacy and sexual leanings. With *The Smiths*, shut-ins, book-readers and outsiders found the music to soundtrack their lives.

BLONDIE
Parallel Lines

Released: September 1978

Label: Chrysalis

Producer: Mike Chapman

Listen: 'Heart of Glass', 'One Way or Another', 'Picture This', 'Hanging on the Telephone', 'Sunday Girl'

Chart placing: US Billboard chart #6, UK chart #1

Trivia: Bona fide chart smash 'Heart of Glass' was a slow reggae shuffle until producer Mike Chapman suggested speeding it up and giving it a disco beat. The song reached number one in more than 10 countries. The 'pain in the ass' line was omitted from the 7-inch version of the track.

Also listen: *Blondie, Plastic Letters, Eat to the Beat, Autoamerican*

✖ DESPITE THEIR PUNK CREDENTIALS, Blondie were more interested in playing with genres than being confined to a rigid aesthetic. This meant taking in elements of pop, disco and '50s and '60s rock 'n' roll, all mashed up in punk's manic blender. Honing their sound on their self-titled debut LP and the follow-up, *Plastic Letters*, Blondie well and truly hit their stride with *Parallel Lines*. The album was an instant smash hit, putting Blondie well and truly on the musical map and spawning several notable singles, including their most recognisable tune, 'Heart of Glass'. Opening salvo 'Hanging on the Telephone' is the archetypal new wave stormer – fast, sexy, catchy, desperate. 'One Way or Another' is a crunchy rocker with a marvellous Debbie Harry vocal and an air of nonchalance and disregard. 'Sunday Girl' and 'Picture This' are both masterclasses in pop, and 'Fade Away and Radiate' catches Blondie in an experimental, almost psychedelic frame of mind. Robert Fripp adds a spiralling guitar line and the song's reggae denouement hints at future Blondie musical territory. *Parallel Lines* showed how true you could be to your sound while still going on to sell 20 million records.

SIOUXSIE AND THE BANSHEES
The Scream

Released: November 1978

Label: Polydor

Producers: Steve Lillywhite, Siouxsie and the Banshees

Listen: 'Overground', 'Mirage', 'Metal Postcard'

Chart Placing: UK chart #12

Trivia: BBC Radio 1 DJ John Peel played the album from start to finish on his show (from cassette tape), one month before its release.

Also listen: *Join Hands, Kaleidoscope, Juju, A Kiss in the Dreamhouse*

✖ SEEN AS A POTENTIAL 'female Sex Pistol', Siouxsie would confound all expectations with her band's debut LP, *The Scream*. Punk may have set the stage, but there was something else happening here: a dark, twisted fairytale – punk, Gothic and bleak – with shades of pre-war German Kabarett and Parisian Grand Guignol. Angular, brittle guitars clash over cavernous drums (heavy on the tom toms) under Siouxsie's manic, confrontational delivery. Recorded in one week, the album's rawness and immediacy give it much of its strength. Single 'Hong Kong Garden' smashed into the charts while the album was being made, but wasn't included on the original version of it. *The Scream* sketched an alien suburban sprawl where darkness gathered in drab corners, with lyrical intensity inspired by literature and music that drew on film scores. Its fans include Peter Hook (Joy Division and New Order) and Jim Reid (The Jesus and Mary Chain) who has said, '"Jigsaw Feeling" from *The Scream* album … that's a reason why I made music'. Other fans include Morrissey, and musician, engineer and producer Steve Albini.

TALKING HEADS
Remain in Light

Released: 8 October 1980

Label: Sire

Producer: Brian Eno

Listen: 'Once in a Lifetime',
'Cross-eyed and Painless',
'Houses in Motion',
'Born Under Punches', 'The Overload'

Chart Placing: US Billboard
chart #19, UK chart #21

Trivia: The iconic cover of *Remain in Light* is thought to be one of the very first record sleeves to use computer-generated graphics. Band members Chris Frantz and Tina Weymouth consulted with MIT researcher Walter Bender, using an extensive computer mainframe (that filled several rooms) to plot out images of the band members in masks.

Also listen: *More Songs about Buildings and Food, Fear of Music*

✖ AT ITS HEART a post-punk album, *Remain in Light* draws influences from psychedelia, world music, the work of Afro-beat star Fela Kuti and avant-garde music, creating art rock in the process. Producer Brian Eno's masterful approach to *Remain in Light* involved drawing on African rhythms, electronica and funk and creating a series of grooves which were repeated, allowing the band to fully collaborate by writing and playing their parts over the top of the looped beats. Musically angular, rhythmic and infectious, the album still stands out for frontman David Byrne's lyrical style and delivery. Using cut-ups and stream of consciousness (Eno had pioneered these styles while working with Bowie) and drawing on rap and African literature, preaching and speech delivery, Byrne built a lyrical landscape that dismantled the American Dream and the human proclivity to semi-sleepwalk through life. 'Once in a Lifetime' is a tour de force, a bona fide post-punk classic, while 'The Overload' was the closest America would come to aping Joy Division until Interpol came onto the scene.

JOHN FOXX
Metamatic

Released: 18 January 1980
Label: Virgin
Producer: John Foxx
Listen: 'Underpass', 'No One Driving', 'He's a Liquid'
Chart placing: UK chart #18

Trivia: Foxx had performed 'Touch and Go' and 'He's a Liquid' when he was with Ultravox. Likewise, Ultravox used 'Touch and Go' as a basis for their track 'Mr. X' on the 1980 album *Vienna*. John Foxx commented on this in 2018, saying, 'Oh, impossible to untangle who did what after you've been in the studio together ...'

Also listen: *The Garden, The Golden Section*

✖ **FOR HIS DEBUT ALBUM** as a solo artist, John Foxx, former lead singer of Ultravox, moved away from his blending of guitar rock and keyboards to craft an eerie slice of urban noir made entirely with synthesisers. Along with Kraftwerk, The Human League and Gary Numan, Foxx was one of the first musicians to use synthesisers to write songs; up to that point they had been used almost exclusively as an accompaniment to traditional instruments, or to make soundtracks. Foxx used the synthesiser as a backing band, which gave him almost complete control over his work. The result was a new sound – melodic songs with alien soundscapes and crisp, haunting melody lines. 'Underpass' was a chart hit, with a brooding, modulated introduction leading into a catchy synth hook line. Foxx was inspired by kinetic art, writer J. G. Ballard's bleak landscapes of suburban decay and noir cinema. *Metamatic* evoked empty high-rise buildings and looming freeways; pristine, clinical shopping centres; people indistinct from robots. Its dystopian visions were hauntingly familiar, but exciting, visceral and new, and inspired a generation of bedroom producers and musicians who would use a punk attitude to manipulate an evolving technology and spawn myriad electronic music scenes.

PUBLIC IMAGE LTD
PUBLIC IMAGE:
First Issue

Released: 8 December 1978
Label: Virgin
Producer: Public Image Ltd
Listen: 'Public Image', 'Low Life',
'Religion I', 'Religion II'
Chart placing: UK chart #22

Trivia: Final track 'Fodderstompf' is
a complete piss-take and the band
admit it. Lydon needed to fill eight
minutes and he did so by spouting
unpleasantries about love and what
a waste of time the song was. It's all
held together by a killer Jah Wobble
bass groove. Lydon said, 'You should've
seen Branson's face when he heard
that, he was furious!'

Also listen: *Metal Box, The Flowers
of Romance, This is What You Want …
This is What You Get*

✖ **NOT CONTENT** with being highly
influential in punk, John Lydon also
thought he'd set about creating post-
punk. Public Image Ltd's first LP did
just that. It took punk's freedoms and
used them to create a primal howl
of discontent and disillusionment,
a reflection of Lydon's disgust with
the music industry and the cult of
'labels' but also, more poignantly,
his disillusionment with the Sex Pistols.
Leading single 'Public Image' addressed
this directly. Lydon described it as 'a
slagging of the group I used to be
in … They never bothered to listen to
what I was fucking singing, they don't
even know the words to my songs …
The rest of the band and Malcolm never
bothered to find out if I could sing,
they just took me as an image.' 'Public
Image' went into the singles chart at
number nine. Lydon said the song 'Low
Life' could have been about McLaren,
but ultimately it was about Sid (Vicious)
and how he turned into the 'worst
kind of rock 'n' roll star'. 'Religion'
was a visceral attack on religion and
religious institutions. Showing that Lydon
hadn't lost any fans, the album went to
number 22 and stayed in the charts for
11 weeks.

DEVO
Q: Are We Not Men?
A: We Are Devo!

Released: September 1978

Label: Warner Brothers, Virgin

Producer: Brian Eno, uncredited input by David Bowie

Listen: 'Mongoloid', 'Gut Feeling', '(I Can't Get No) Satisfaction', 'Jocko Homo'

Chart placing: US Billboard chart #78, UK chart #12

Trivia: The music video for 'Mongoloid' featured groundbreaking use of collage by American avant-garde visual artist Bruce Connor, who combined found footage from sci-fi clips, TV ads and science documentaries from the '50s to which he added his own film work and animation.

Also listen: *Duty Now for the Future, Freedom of Choice*

✖ **BOWIE AND ENO EXPRESSED** interest in producing Devo's first album after hearing a demo. Eno set about putting the album together in Cologne at Conny Plank's Studio, with help from Bowie 'on the weekends', as Simon Reynolds put it in *Rip It Up and Start Again*. Devo were resistant to Eno's ideas, keen to preserve the original sound and feel of their demo. The title is Devo's response to the question 'Are we not men?' posed by a character in H. G. Wells' *The Island of Doctor Moreau*. At times the album is an uncomfortable listen. 'Mongoloid' describes the life of a man hiding his Down syndrome so that he can live a 'normal' life. The buzzing guitars and stop-start chorus make it disconcerting yet oddly catchy. The cover of The Rolling Stones' '(I Can't Get No) Satisfaction' is twitchy and mechanical. In 'Uncontrollable Urge', 'Jocko Homo' and 'Gut Feeling' the band navigate the treacherous waters of adolescence. Although initial critical and commercial reaction was mixed, the deadpan, robotic delivery, unusual time signatures and irony were unique and highly influential on new wave, post-punk, art rock and electronica.

THE HUMAN LEAGUE
Dare

Released: 16 October 1981

Label: Virgin

Producers: Martin Rushent, The Human League

Listen: 'Don't You Want Me', 'Open Your Heart', 'Love Action', 'Sound of the Crowd'

Chart placing: UK chart #1

Trivia: *Dare* was Virgin Records' first number one album (and single with 'Don't You Want Me') since its first release, Mike Oldfield's *Tubular Bells*, in 1973. A delighted Richard Branson sent Oakey a motorcycle as a gift.

Also listen: 'Reproduction', 'Travelogue'

✖ AFTER MARTYN WARE and Ian Craig Marsh left the more experimental early version of The Human League to form Heaven 17, Phil Oakey led the band in a new, more accessible direction. *Dare* was a smash hit all over the world, an album crammed with memorable songs, perfectly poised on the brink of the synth-pop revolution in 1981. Miles away from punk, *Dare* was glossy and catchy, but still kept a little mystery at its core. Tracks like 'I Am the Law', 'Darkness' and 'Seconds' lent the album gravitas. 'Sound of the Crowd' is an oddball pop moment, with an off-kilter beat and mash-up 'club poetry' lyrics. 'Don't You Want Me', 'Love Action' and 'Open Your Heart' were chart stormers – electro, singalong ditties about love and loss that heralded the glossy, ambitious '80s. *Dare's* perfect mix of hits and intrigue made it one of the decade's most popular and influential electronic albums. Steve Sutherland wrote in *Melody Maker*, 'Sure to upset some, sell to millions more and so it should, the way it tramps all over rock traditions.' *Dare* stayed in the UK pop charts for a staggering 74 weeks.

TUBEWAY ARMY
Replicas

Released: April 1979
Label: Beggars Banquet
Producer: Gary Numan
Listen: 'Are "Friends" Electric?',
'Down in the Park'
Chart placing: UK chart #1

Trivia: Gary Numan has explained that 'Are "Friends" Electric?' was originally made up of two separate songs and that the keyboard line was 'quite lilting, quite sweet. I just hit the wrong note one day and thought, that sounds better. So I kept it.'

Also listen: *Tubeway Army, The Pleasure Principle, Telekon*

✖ THE SOUND OF *REPLICAS* was born when lead singer Gary Numan stumbled upon a Minimoog in the studio. When he played it (he described it as being like 'ten guitar players hitting one note played with one finger') and the band joined in, they created the perfect post-punk/new wave melange. The legacies of Bowie, Kraftwerk, Ultravox (John Foxx era), Eno, glam rock, sci-fi literature and cinema, and a climate of flourishing technology (and subsequent 'technofear'), fuelled an album of clipped electronica, synth fuzz, crunching guitars and one-note keyboard hooks. Thematically, the album was a paranoid vision of the future, encompassing aliens and alienation, violent entertainment, faceless corporations, and the emptiness brought about by reliance on technology. Lead single 'Are "Friends" Electric?', a song about robot prostitutes, was a number one hit, happily programmed on unwary radio stations and *Top of the Pops*. This paved the way for *Replicas*' success. It was the perfect timing for a record that might otherwise have been considered 'too strange' by the masses. The album influenced electronic and industrial acts and 'Down in the Park' was covered by both the Foo Fighters and Marilyn Manson.

ALSO HIGHLY INFLUEN-TIAL

Pere Ubu
'30 Seconds Over Tokyo' (song)

Talk Talk
It's My Life

The Psychedelic Furs
Talk Talk Talk

Magazine
Real Life

Depeche Mode
Speak and Spell

The Fall
Live at the Witch Trials

Yazoo
Upstairs at Eric's

Cocteau Twins
Garlands

Echo & the Bunnymen
Porcupine

Ian Dury
New Boots and Panties!!

New Order
Movement

Oingo Boingo
Only a Lad

The Pop Group
Y

The Residents
Meet the Residents

Heaven 17
Penthouse and Pavement

Japan
Gentlemen Take Polaroids

The Birthday Party
Prayers on Fire

Soft Cell
Non-Stop Erotic Cabaret

Elvis Costello
This Year's Model

The B-52's
The B-52's

ABC
The Lexicon of Love

Laurie Anderson
Big Science

Blancmange
Happy Families

Simple Minds
Sons and Fascination

Buggles
The Age of Plastic

Vapours
New Clear Days

The Church
Of Skins and Heart

XTC
Drums and Wires

Sparks
Kimono My House

Wall of Voodoo
Dark Continent

Tears for Fears
The Hurting

Thomas Dolby
The Golden Age of Wireless

The Cars
Candy-O

Fad Gadget
Fireside Favourites

The Go-Betweens
Before Hollywood

Post-Punk & New Wave:

The artists.

Devo

Devo formed in Akron, Ohio in 1972. The band was made up of two sets of brothers, Mark and Bob Mothersbaugh and Gerald and Bob Casale, who were joined by Alan Myers on drums. Gerald Casale and fellow art student at Kent State University, Bob Lewis, developed a comical theory, 'De-Evolution', in which mankind had reached 'peak culture' and had started to regress rather than evolve. The theory gave the band its name and its own manifesto. Way before slacker or geek rock, Devo were launching their own revenge of the nerds. The music dealt with science fiction and fact, the social underbelly and the dissolution of the American dream. With a theatrical stage show, quirky movements, songs laced with humour and, of course, the famous Devo 'energy dome' helmets, Devo were often considered comical. Their first two LPs, Q: Are We Not Men? A: We Are Devo! and Duty Now For the Future, created disconcerting soundscapes of jerky rock, obscure time signatures and perverse lyrics. They would later achieve mainstream success with songs like 'Whip It', 'Freedom of Choice' and 'Beautiful World'. The nerds' revenge was complete.

Mark Bob Gerald & Bob

Mark Mothersbaugh formed the company Mutato Muzika, which produces soundtracks for film and television. Having suffered from myopia and astigmatism from the age of seven, Mothersbaugh later developed his own range of glasses with eyewear company Shane Baum.

The Devo 'energy dome' helmet, also known as the 'flowerpot hat', was introduced around the time of the release of 'Freedom of Choice' in 1980. Mark Mothersbaugh said, 'We were influenced by the German Bauhaus movement, geometric fashion and Aztec temples. We just liked the look …' Gerald Casale said that the domes 'increased mental energy'. Devo appeared in an ad for Diet Coke in 1984 wearing white versions of the helmet.

Gerald Casale was one of the pioneers of the pop music video, directing most of Devo's clips as well as the videos for Silverchair's 'Freak' and the Foo Fighters' 'I'll Stick Around'.

Devo have stated that although the idea of 'De-Evolution' was initially a joke, when the Kent State shootings happened on 4 May 1973, killing four students, they resolved to form a band that highlighted the disintegration of society.

Devo released *The Truth About De-Evolution* in 1976. Directed by Chuck Statler, the film won first prize at the Ann Arbor Film Festival. It was essentially made up of two clips for the songs 'Secret Agent Man' and 'Jocko Homo'.

Joy
Division

Bernard Sumner wrote in his autobiography, 'Joy Division sounded like Manchester: cold, sparse and at times, bleak.' Johnny Marr of The Smiths said, 'They sounded like the place they came from, without a doubt.'

Joy Division formed in Salford, northern England, in 1978. As was the case for many bands at the time, a Sex Pistols gig inspired them to play music. Guitarist Bernard Sumner stated that the Pistols 'destroyed the myth of being a pop star'. Sumner and bass player Peter Hook recruited Ian Curtis as lead vocalist. They named their band Warsaw, after Bowie's 'Warszawa', from the album *Low*. Drummer Stephen Morris soon joined, and the band renamed themselves Joy Division. Tony Wilson, head of Factory Records, signed them to the label. After a gig at Manchester's Rafters club, the venue's resident DJ, Rob Gretton, convinced the band to take him on as manager. Joy Division recorded pivotal post-punk album *Unknown Pleasures* in April 1979. Producer Martin Hannett took the band's dense, bass-heavy live sound and added atmosphere and space. The band were unimpressed at the time, but Hook later commented that Hannett had 'created the Joy Division sound'. *Unknown Pleasures* was confrontational, abrasive, challenging and imbued with desperation, darkness and an almost spiritual transcendence. The band toured with the Buzzcocks and released the single 'Transmission', which garnered them a following of brooding, ardent young intellectuals in overcoats. They successfully toured Europe and recorded their second album, *Closer*. Curtis was struggling with a failing marriage, depression, possible bipolar disorder and extreme bouts of epilepsy, some of which occurred on stage. Finding everything overwhelming, he took his life on 18 May 1980, on the eve of the band's first American tour. The band posthumously released *Closer* and their best-known single, 'Love Will Tear Us Apart'. Unable to go on as Joy Division, the remaining members renamed themselves New Order; the band went on to become hugely successful and highly influential.

The night before he hanged himself in the kitchen, Curtis had watched Werner Herzog's tragic comedy-drama *Stroszek*, about a German musician who moves to America but ends up committing suicide when betrayed by his girlfriend. He also listened to Iggy Pop's *The Idiot*. In her memoir *Touching From a Distance*, Deborah Curtis recalls how Ian asked her to drop the divorce, but also admitted that he was still seeing his lover, Annik Honoré. Deborah found Ian's body at their house on the morning of 18 May 1980. She said that he wrote a long letter to her and mentioned that he wished he was dead, but she didn't regard it to be a suicide note.

Ian
Bernard
Peter
& Stephen

Despite many warning signs, band and management were shocked by Curtis' death. Peter Hook said, 'There were just too many Ians to cope with.' Journalist Paul Morley described *Closer* as a 'series of blatant suicide notes to a number of people in Ian's immediate vicinity'.

The name Joy Division was bleak and dark, like much of the band's music. Taken from the book *House of Dolls* by Ka-Tzetnik 135633, it was the name for the sexual slavery wing of a Nazi concentration camp.

The Smiths

The antithesis of chart pop, The Smiths would be lumped with the 'miserablist' tag, as many considered Morrissey's lyrics dark and depressing. This annoyed BBC Radio 1 announcer John Peel no end. He said, 'On more than one occasion I've actually laughed out loud at The Smiths' lyrics, and I don't often do that ... I don't see them as miserable at all and I get rather cross when people tell me they are.'

The Smiths formed in Manchester in 1982 with Morrissey on vocals, Johnny Marr on guitar, Andy Rourke on bass and Mike Joyce on drums. The Morrissey/Marr songwriting partnership was effectively the 'alternative' Lennon/McCartney: they were a defiant unit who were 'standing up for the gawk', in the words of Johnny Marr. In bookish, shy, rake-skinny Morrissey, a generation now had a defender. His image – hearing aid, National Health glasses and a bouquet of gladioli sprouting from his back pocket – is now the stuff of legend. Meanwhile, Marr shimmied about the stage with floppy hair, leather jacket and beads, peeling out killer guitar riffs that jangled their way into the subconscious of discerning listeners. Lyrically, there were arresting, dark Manchester-centric vignettes about the likes of the Moors Murders, and cautionary tales about the intricacies, insecurities and often soul-destroying aspects of relationships. Having burst out of the bedroom, the fans were jubilant, defiant and aggressively proud of being a square peg in a round hole. Expected to sign to Factory Records, although the band maintain that they never had the intention, the ever-contrary Smiths went instead with London's Rough Trade. In a short space of time – some five years – The Smiths released four genre-defining albums and a slew of popular singles that would see them placed forever in the timeline of influential and popular underground bands. Their second LP, *Meat Is Murder*, dealt unabashedly with topics as far-ranging as corporal punishment, loneliness and the inherent cruelty in meat consumption. Third LP *The Queen Is Dead* was a huge commercial success and a breakthrough for a band that had already drawn an army of followers. Having released many excellent non-album singles, The Smiths also put out two great 'collections', including the exceptional Hatful of Hollow. It all added up to an extraordinary output over a short space of time, and a canon of songs that continue to gather popularity to this day. The band broke up in 1987 over musical differences and personality clashes. Morrissey and Marr went on to have successful careers outside of the band.

Bass player Andy Rourke was sacked from the band just after the release of The Queen is Dead, due to a spiralling heroin addiction. Although Morrissey denies it, Rourke says that he was fired via a Post-it note stuck to his car window that read, 'Andy you have left the Smiths — goodbye and good luck, Morrissey'. Rourke was replaced by Craig Gannon, who then moved to rhythm guitar when Rourke was reinstated a mere two weeks later.

Morrissey Johnny — Mike & Andy

Morrissey said, on choosing The Smiths as a band name, 'It was the most ordinary name and I thought it was time that the ordinary folk of the world showed their faces.'

In 1989 Rourke and Joyce began a legal dispute over royalties. They had initially agreed to a deal giving them 10 per cent performance and writing royalties each, with Morrissey and Marr getting 40 per cent each. Joyce and Rourke argued that they were more than just session musicians. Eventually, Joyce received £1,000,000 in back royalties and a 25 per cent ongoing split. Rourke received a smaller amount in an out-of-court settlement. He declared bankruptcy in 1999. The judge on the case famously described Morrissey as 'devious and truculent'. Morrissey said afterwards, 'To me, the Smiths were a beautiful thing and Johnny left it, and Mike has destroyed it.' His track 'Sorrow Will Come in the End' on solo album Maladjusted deals aggressively with the issue.

The Smiths broke up in 1987, prior to the release of their most successful album, Strangeways, Here We Come, which reached number two on the UK chart and number 55 in America. The relationship between Morrissey and Marr had broken down. Morrissey said it was because Marr was working with too many other artists, but later admitted the lack of a manager and business problems were behind the split. Marr openly despised Morrissey covering '60s pop artists. He said, 'That was the last straw, really. I didn't form a group to perform Cilla Black songs.'

The Cure

The Cure formed in Crawley, West Sussex, in 1978, with Robert Smith on vocals, 'Lol' Tolhurst on drums, Mick Dempsey on guitar and Simon Gallup on bass. After releasing their debut album *Three Imaginary Boys* in 1979, the band supported Siouxsie and the Banshees. The experience was pivotal for Smith. When the American version of their debut, dubbed *Boys Don't Cry*, was released, The Cure gained worldwide attention. They had already had a number of up-tempo hits in the charts when, according to an interview in *Guitar World* magazine, Smith chanced to see the band Wire playing live. After this, The Cure changed direction, moving from spiky punk-pop to the brittle, atmospheric, immersive, minimal sound heard on *Seventeen Seconds* and *Faith*. The band nevertheless continued to have chart hits in the atmospheric 'A Forest', despair-laden 'Primary' and proto-Gothic gloom anthem 'Charlotte Sometimes'. The Cure would go on to complete their neo-Gothic triptych with the almost impenetrable, paranoid confessional of *Pornography*. These releases remain influential today for their starkness and honesty, and spawned a generation of bands bent on making their own form of confessional post-punk. On the brink of a psychotic breakdown and with the collapse of the band apparently imminent, Robert Smith 'retooled' The Cure, and went on to conquer the world with a string of catchy chart singles, all imbued with 'Cure cute'. Smith strutted about, a player on a fantastical stage, all smudged lipstick and fright-wig hair, gathering an army of fans and inspiring a generation of imitators. The band would revisit their darker side from time to time, especially on eighth studio LP and fan favourite *Disintegration*, and blend it with melodic, quirky, off-kilter, disjointed pop. The Cure are among the progenitors of alternative rock and helped spawn a range of genres including Goth, alt-pop, emo, industrial and shoegaze.

The Cure started their career called The Obelisk and Easy Cure.

Robert Lol Mick & Simon

On their fifth album, *The Top*, released in 1984, Smith played all instruments except for the drums.

The title of The Cure's debut single, 'Killing an Arab', naturally caused controversy. It was inspired by Albert Camus' novel *L'Étranger*, but this didn't stop the band from having to fend of accusations of racism. The band placed a sticker on the re-released 7-inch single and on the 1986 compilation *Standing On A Beach*, denying the racist connotations.

In a classic sequence in *The Mighty Boosh*'s Goth-tinged episode 'Nanageddon', Vince Noir (Noel Fielding) produces the hairspray with the most powerful hold known to man, saying it was 'made from the tears of Robert Smith'. *South Park* also featured a classic Robert Smith episode, in which character Cartman calls *Disintegration* the 'best album ever'.

Tim Pope directed the majority of The Cure's videos, beginning with 'Let's Go to Bed' in 1982. Pope said he wanted to bring out their 'playfulness'. He said, 'The Cure is the ultimate band for a filmmaker to work with because Old Smiffy really understands the camera. His songs are so cinematic.'

Wire

Wire have been cited as a major influence on a wide range of artists including Sonic Youth, Henry Rollins, REM, Ladytron, Helmet, Franz Ferdinand and My Bloody Valentine. Robert Smith said The Cure changed their sound after he saw Wire play live.

Wire are a four piece formed in London in 1976. The core line-up was Colin Newman on guitar and vocals, Graham Lewis on bass and vocals, Robert Grey on drums and Bruce Gilbert on guitar (Gilbert left in 2004). Despite achieving limited sales and commercial attention, Wire are one of the most influential bands to come out of the punk era. At publication time the band have released an impressive 17 albums, with significant time passing between 1979's 154 and 1987's The Ideal Copy, and 1991's The First Letter (released under the name Wir) and 2003's Send. Wire covered all angles of the post-punk landscape on their first three albums. Pink Flag was released in the midst of the UK punk explosion and while it sat happily in the punk genre, it expanded on the limited punk palette, bringing in harsher guitar sounds, lo-fi production, melodic guitar lines and intelligent lyrics. The album was a major influence on post-punk and hardcore punk. Chairs Missing anticipated art rock, new wave, Britpop and indie jangle with its forward-looking sounds and more in-depth song structures and lyrics. Longer, more intricate songs distanced the band from punk. 154 experimented even further, consolidating the band's influence on future alternative pop, avant pop, art rock, minimalism and more. A Bell is a Cup ... Until it is Struck (1988), Red Barked Tree (2010) and Change Becomes Us (2013) are high points in an impressive resume, showing the band's maturing sound and ability to create warmth and texture.

Colin Graham Robert & Bruce

Graham Lewis described the name Wire as 'being chosen for its graphic quality ... it was short and stark and would look big on a poster, even if we were low on the bill!'.

Smiths guitarist Johnny Marr was a fan of Wire. He said, 'They [Wire] sounded like Wire being as great as they can be ... that was quite a profound revelation to me.' Before Marr embarked on his true solo career in 2013, he realised he could 'just be me as well as I can possibly be', exploring a world of possibilities within a narrow remit.

It's not hard to see the influence of Wire tune 'Three Girl Rhumba' on Britpop band Elastica's mega hit 'Connection'. Wire described it as 'ripped off', but an out-of-court settlement and change in credits resolved the issue.

Gang of Four

Gang of Four formed in the fine art department of Leeds University. The department also spawned bands The Mekons and Delta 5.

Gang of Four formed in Leeds in 1976. The band consisted of Jon King on vocals, Andy Gill on guitar, Dave Allen on bass and Hugo Burnham on drums. With music that was disjointed, monotone, nihilistic and repetitive, Gang of Four took punk's DIY, anything-goes attitude and shaped a new sound. Their unapologetically left-wing politics and social commentary set them up as more cerebral than most punk bands. Andy Gill described the band's sound as having been driven by 'living in a late capitalist society' and said they were 'very concerned about the spectre of Thatcherism, and what it was going to do to the people'. All that angst and deep thinking didn't mean they couldn't lay down a groove, however. Gang of Four's social and political commentary was layered over angular beats, funk rhythms and sparse, robotic instrumentation. Earnest young intellectuals and bedroom rebels had a band they could champion before their adulation would turn towards Joy Division and The Smiths. Artists who have name-checked Gang of Four include REM, Flea from Red Hot Chili Peppers, Kurt Cobain and later Franz Ferdinand, Bloc Party and The Rapture. The original line-up reunited between 2004 and 2006, although post 2011 Andy Gill would be the only original member in the band. Gill died from pneumonia at the age of sixty-four on 1 February 2020.

Despite being an underground band, Gang of Four had a surprise pop hit in 1982 with 'I Love A Man in Uniform', which reached number 27 on the US dance club chart. In 1983 their track 'Is it Love' breached the top 10 of the same chart.

Gail Ann Dorsey, bass player in Bowie's band from 1995 until his death in 2016, appeared as a bass player in various line-ups for Gang of Four over the years and sang guest vocals on 'First World Citizen', on their 2015 album, *What Happens Next*.

Talking about their sound, Andy Gill said, 'Instead of guitar solos we had anti solos, where you stopped playing, just left a hole … valve amps were verboten … I had transistorised amps, a more brittle, cleaner sound. Gang of Four were against warmth.'

Jon
Andy
Dave
& Hugo

Orchestral Manoeuvres in the Dark

Formed in Wirral in northern England in 1978, Orchestral Manoeuvres in the Dark (often abbreviated to OMD) were made up of core members Andy McCluskey on bass and vocals and Paul Humphreys on vocals and keyboards, embellished by Stuart Kershaw on drums and Martin Cooper on keyboards and saxophone. The quintessential new wave 'synth' band, OMD used guitars sparingly (McCluskey's bass was a constant, however) and crafted songs and soundscapes with the use of the developing electronic keyboards, in particular the Fairlight, an early sampler that let you record a sound and then transpose it over the keyboard. They used technology but their music was warm, human and emotional, in part due to an astounding ear for melody and McCluskey's vocals, which could go from honey and velvet to a dissonant howl within the same track. The self-titled debut album sat perfectly between post-punk and new wave, with killer keyboard hooks and jaunty beats clashing with abrasive sounds and disorienting time signatures. The next three albums remain their masterworks. *Organisation, Architecture & Morality* and *Dazzle Ships* had enough hits to stalk the upper reaches of the charts – 'Enola Gay', 'Souvenir', 'Joan of Arc (Maid of Orleans)', 'Locomotion', 'Telegraph'. But OMD also wanted to play around with the form – they experimented with sounds and beats, cut-ups, tape loops and found sounds. This was particularly evident on *Dazzle Ships*. OMD would go on to release several strong albums through the '80s and have a few more mega-hits, including perennial favourite 'If You Leave' (a US Billboard top 10 hit thanks in part to its inclusion on the *Pretty in Pink* soundtrack) and 'Forever Live and Die'. The group disbanded for a while, then reunited in the 2010s and have released three more albums to date.

During OMD's hiatus after 1988, Andy McCluskey continued as a solo act under the OMD name. He had a successful chart single with 'Sailing on the Seven Seas' from the album *Sugar Tax*, both of which reached number 3 in the UK chart. After this McCluskey ended this iteration of OMD to found and write material for Liverpool girl group Atomic Kitten. He co-wrote their number 1 hit, 'Whole Again', with Stuart Kershaw from OMD and pop songwriters Bill Padley and Jeremy Godfrey.

Andy Paul Stuart & Martin

Despite being a huge, bouncy pop hit with a killer keyboard riff, 'Enola Gay' deals with some serious subject matter. Enola Gay was the name of the aeroplane that dropped the atomic bomb on Hiroshima. The line, 'Is mother proud of little boy today' refers to the bomb, which the Americans had called 'Little Boy'. OMD liked to smuggle dark or political subjects into the charts, hiding them in plain sight.

Joan of Arc (*Maid of Orleans*) was the biggest-selling single in Germany in 1982.

OMD were interested in anthropomorphism, the practice of giving animals or objects human qualities.

Fine examples of this are 'Enola Gay' and 'Stanlow', where they refer to objects and buildings as 'you',

imbue them with feelings and allow them emotional interactions.

Talking Heads

Although they were part of the CBGB and punk scene, Talking Heads were always considered outsiders. Punk bands were dishevelled, angry, unwashed and uncultured. Talking Heads were clean-cut, liked disco and funk and were decidedly non-rock. David Byrne said of punk, 'Stage postures and all those inherited gestures … I thought it wasn't saying anything new … I thought, let's see if we can just throw all that out, start from square one.'

David Byrne and Brian Eno worked extensively together. Eno had always had trouble writing lyrics, and together with Byrne discovered that modes of speech could influence lyrics and vocals. They became extremely interested in speeches given by revivalist Christian preachers, describing their manner of talking as melodic and rhythmical. This influence is clear on the Byrne/Eno collaboration *My Life in the Bush of Ghosts* and Talking Heads' *Remain in Light*.

After *Remain in Light* Weymouth said, 'Talking Heads spent so many years trying to be original, that we don't know what is original anymore.'

David
Chris
Tina
& Jerry

Tina Weymouth and Chris Frantz's side project Tom Tom Club released an eponymous album in 1981 that spawned two hits, 'Wordy Rappinghood' and 'Genius of Love'. 'Wordy Rappinghood' was inspired in part by Moroccan children's song called 'A Ram Sam Sam'.

The name Talking Heads came from TV studio 'head and shoulders' shots of people talking. Weymouth said the name fit as it implied 'all talk, no action'.

Talking Heads formed in 1975 in New York City. The band consisted of David Byrne on vocals and guitar, Tina Weymouth on bass, Chris Frantz on drums and Jerry Harrison on keyboards and guitar. They fused punk, art rock, funk and world music to forge a new sound. A unique approach to lyrics and vocal delivery saw them become one of the most important and influential bands in the American new wave movement. Talking Heads will be forever linked with art rock and, in fact, Byrne, Weymouth and Frantz had all attended the Rhode Island School of Design. Byrne and Frantz had even been in a band called The Artistics. It took just one element to convert that earnest approach into something new and vital, and that was punk. Living communally in New York City, the three became obsessed with the punk scene. Jerry Harrison came to the band via a punk band, The Modern Lovers. Art, books, cinema and experimentalism collided with the raw energy and DIY ethic of punk rock, and Talking Heads were born. Their debut LP was released on Sire Records and garnered them an instant following and their first hit, 'Psycho Killer'. Follow-up album *More Songs About Buildings and Food* gave them another hit in their cover of Al Green's 'Take Me to the River'. *Fear of Music* (1979) continues to be highly regarded to this day and showed that Talking Heads had well and truly settled into their sound. *Remain in Light* followed, with its worldwide hit 'Once in a Lifetime'. A string of popular singles, like 'And She Was' and 'Road to Nowhere', added commercial success to existing credibility.

Blondie

Blondie were originally called Angel and the Snake.

Single 'Rapture', from Blondie's 1980 album *Autoamerican*, was the first song featuring rap vocals

to reach number one on the US chart.

Debbie Harry was the centrefold in issue 4 of New York's *Punk* magazine.

Debbie Chris Clem Jimmy & Gary

Debbie Harry and guitarist Chris Stein met when they were both in the Stilettoes. They were together until 1989. During that time Harry said they were drug users but eventually went into rehab and got clean. Harry took time off to look after Stein, who suffered from pemphigus, an autoimmune condition that causes blisters and sores on the skin.

Debbie Harry's birth name is Angela Trimble, but when she was three months of age Richard and Catherine Harry adopted her. Before forming Blondie, Harry worked as a model, a waitress at Max's Kansas City, a secretary at the New York office of the BBC, a go-go dancer and a Playboy Bunny. She performed as back-up singer in folk band the Wind in the Willows before joining the Stilettoes, who then recruited Stein.

Blondie were both integral to and set apart from the punk scene. They didn't quite fit the mould. Visually they had it down, and like the Ramones they borrowed from, and messed with, '50s and '60s pop music tropes. Vocalist Debbie Harry and guitarist Chris Stein formed the band in the mid 1970s, recruiting Clem Burke on drums, Jimmy Destri on keyboards and Gary Valentine on bass. Considered an underground band in America (until the release of *Parallel Lines*), Blondie were popular in Australia and the UK from the beginning, due in part to their new wave sound, which was yet to truly take off in the US. Debbie Harry became a punk style icon almost immediately, adopting a look that combined androgyny, torn clothes, bin bags, fetish gear and thrift-store chic, all worn with a louche insouciance and set off by bleached blonde hair that deliberately had the regrowth showing. Blondie's self-titled debut album was released in 1976 but was largely ignored. Things turned around for Blondie when Australian television presenter Ian 'Molly' Meldrum accidentally played the B-side of the single 'X Offender', 'In The Flesh'. The single went to number two. A successful tour of Australia followed and the world started to take notice. *Plastic Letters* came out in in 1978, spawned the hit 'Denis' and reached number 10 on the UK chart. Third album *Parallel Lines* (1978) was a massive hit, reaching number one in the UK and number six in the States. Follow-ups *Eat to the Beat* and *Autoamerican* were also successful, taking Blondie well and truly out of punk, through new wave and into the mainstream.

John Foxx's *The Garden* featured a track called 'Systems of Romance', written for but not included on the Ultravox album of the same name. 'The Garden' became the name of Foxx's new recording studio.

John Foxx /Ultravox

Before Midge Ure led Ultravox to the top of the charts with seminal New Romantic album *Vienna*, and the subsequent worldwide hit single of the same name, Ultravox were led by electronic pioneer John Foxx and released three studio albums and a compilation,1979's *Three Into One*. The band formed in 1973, and was made up of lead singer Foxx (Dennis Leigh), Stevie Shears on guitars, Warren Cann on drums, Billy Currie on violin and Chris Cross (born Christopher Allen) on bass. Fans of Bowie, Eno and Roxy Music, the New York Dolls and Kraftwerk, they came up with a unique sound that blended punk; bleak, dystopian rock; glam; space rock; and pop noir, predicting post-punk and new wave. The band released three LPs with heavyweight producers like Eno, Conny Plank and Steve Lillywhite. John Foxx was a strip-skinny, angular front man with a delivery that veered between ominous roboticness and punky exuberance. The first two LPs, *Ultravox!* and *Ha! Ha! Ha!*, had limited success despite critical acclaim and BBC airplay. *Ha! Ha! Ha!* featured the song 'Hiroshima Mon Amour', a prototype for synth pop and '80s electronica. Follow-up album *Systems of Romance* came out in 1978, and made greater use of the synthesiser. It also failed to achieve much success, and in the ensuing months tensions simmered over within the band and John Foxx left. Remaining members Warren Cann and Billy Currie recruited Midge Ure as singer. Ure had met Currie when they both worked on the first two Visage albums with Steve Strange. With Chris Cross on bass and keyboards they went on to have a successful run of hit singles and albums, including *Vienna*, *Rage in Eden* and *Quartet*. Foxx released seminal electronic album *Metamatic* and a dreamy slice of New Romantic pop called *The Garden*, whose title track was one of the highlights of the synth-dominated early '80s. John Foxx continues to work in the field of experimental electronica today.

John Stevie Billy Warren & Chris

After releasing the albums *The Golden Section* and *Mysterious Ways*, Foxx left music to pursue a career in graphic design, which included teaching. Foxx designed covers for Jeanette Winterson's *Sexing The Cherry* and Salman Rushdie's *The Moor's Last Sigh*. He returned to music in the early 90s, inspired by ambient music and experimental electronica.

Towards the end of his time with Ultravox (apart from a later reunion) and before embarking on a solo career, Midge Ure co-wrote the charity single 'Do They Know It's Christmas?' with Bob Geldof for the Band Aid project. He also produced the track.

Ultravox were originally called Tiger Lily, which they settled on after going through a few names, including The Zips, Fire of London and The Damned, which they dropped when they found out another band was using it …

Japan formed in 1974 in Catford, a district in south-east London, and featured David Sylvian (David Batt) on vocals, Steve Jansen on drums, Richard Barbieri on keyboards and Mick Karn (Andonis Michaelides) on bass (lead guitarist Rob Dean would join them in 1975). When Japan began their influences stemmed from glam and experimental rock – Roxy Music, Eno, the New York Dolls, The Velvet Underground and T-Rex. Their first two albums, *Adolescent Sex* and *Obscure Alternatives*, both released in 1978, were thought of as slightly passé in a time when punk and new wave were changing the sound of music. On their subsequent releases, the single 'Life in Tokyo' and the album *Quiet Life*, they moved into new wave territory without straying too far from their glamorous yet experimental roots. David Sylvian's androgynous yet masculine look – dyed blonde hair, make-up, expensive suits and crisp, frilled shirts – was highly influential on the burgeoning new wave and '80s synth-pop movements. He held the microphone with his fingertips like a crooner, his baritone honey-and-sandpaper vocals melting over Karn's jaunty slide bass and Jansen and Barbieri's staccato keyboard stings and off-kilter beats. Their two albums for Virgin, *Gentlemen Take Polaroids* and *Tin Drum*, saw them aligned to some extent with the New Romantic movement. After a live album and a best-of collection, Japan split. Sylvian went on to explore ambient music and ballads and continued to experiment with beats and Eastern sounds for three beautiful solo albums, *Brilliant Trees* (number four on the UK chart), *Gone To Earth* and *Secrets of the Beehive*. Mick Karn died of cancer in January 2011.

Japan collaborated with Ryuichi Sakamoto (from highly regarded Japanese electronic band Yellow Magic Orchestra) on the song 'Taking Islands in Africa', from the *Gentlemen Take Polaroids* album. This led to them collaborating on the soundtrack for the 1983 film *Merry Christmas Mr. Lawrence*, resulting in the beautiful single 'Forbidden Colours'.

Japan covered a track on *Adolescent Sex* that pointed to less punk/glam influences – 'Don't Rain on My Parade', from the musical *Funny Girl*. They would later cover Marvin Gaye's 'Ain't That Peculiar' on *Gentlemen Take Polaroids*.

Japan

Japan's debut album, *Adolescent Sex*, was released as a self-titled album in some countries to avoid controversy. Its biggest success was in namesake country Japan, where it went to number 20 on the national chart.

After Japan, Mick Karn formed a band with Pete Murphy of Bauhaus and Paul Vincent Lawford called Dalis Car. They released one album, *The Waking Hour*, in 1984.

The original four members of the band, Sylvian, Karn, Barbieri and Jansen, reunited in 1989 with a new name, Rain Tree Crow. They released a self-titled album in 1991.

David Steve Richard Mick & Rob

Elvis Costello & The Attractions

Elvis Costello & the Attractions replaced the Sex Pistols on *Saturday Night Live* in December 1977. Told to play 'Less Than Zero', they instead played 'Radio Radio', a song that pilloried commercial radio airplay. They were banned from *Saturday Night Live* but their popularity, and sales of the debut album, went crazy.

On *Some Product,* an album of sound bites and interviews, Steve Jones from the Sex Pistols said, 'Elvis Costello … wears glasses with no actual glass in them'.

Elvis Costello was born Declan MacManus in 1954 in Paddington, London. His debut album, *My Aim Is True*, was released through Stiff Records in 1977. Costello's backing band for the debut were an American country music outfit living in London called Clover. For his next single, 'Watching the Detectives', Costello recruited Steve Nieve (Stephen Nason), from Graham Parker and The Rumour, Steve Goulding and Andrew Bodnar. Costello eventually settled on Steve Nieve on keyboards, Bruce Thomas on bass and Pete Thomas on drums. Dubbing them The Attractions, the unit became a pivotal link between punk and new wave. The band wore thin ties and suit jackets, had spiky hair and leapt about the stage like jumping jacks on happy pills. Costello was the perfect anti-idol, with oversized Buddy Holly glasses, a permanent sneer, very 'English' teeth and a pigeon-toed strut. He also had an incredible sense of melody and a penchant for witty wordplay.

Elvis Steve Bruce & Pete

After *Get Happy!!*, Elvis Costello & The Attractions released Trust (1981), *Almost Blue* (1981), *Imperial Bedroom* (1982), *Punch the Clock* (1983) and *Goodbye Cruel World* (1984). Hit singles from these records include 'Good Year for the Roses', 'Everyday I Write the Book', 'Shipbuilding', 'I Just Want to Be Loved' and 'Veronica'. *Almost Blue* consisted mainly of country music covers by artists like Hank Williams and Gram Parsons.

The band would go on to release three albums that took in punk, pop, new wave, country, Northern Soul and even reggae influences. *This Year's Model* (1978) (number four on the UK chart) featured the hits '(I Don't Want to Go to) Chelsea' and 'Pump It Up' ('Watching the Detectives' was added to some releases). *Armed Forces* followed in January 1979, reaching number two on the UK chart and garnering The Attractions a number two single and worldwide hit with 'Oliver's Army'. *Get Happy!!* came out in February 1980, reaching number two in the UK. This was a remarkable feat, as it came just eight months after the previous record and featured 20 songs, all of them excellent. The album took in ska, soul and R&B influences but retained a new wave/punk-pop flavour. Costello went on to release five more albums with The Attractions before pursuing a solo career, where he explored more traditional forms of country music and jazz.

Costello's original backing band Clover featured various musicians who also played with Huey Lewis & the News, The Doobie Brothers, Toto and Lucinda Williams.

Depeche Mode

Inspired by OMD, The Human League, Fad Gadget and The Normal, Clarke and Fletcher started exclusively playing the synthesiser.

The band named themselves after French fashion magazine *Depeche Mode*. Gore said, 'It means fast fashion, or fashion dispatch. I like the sound of that.'

Depeche Mode formed in Basildon, Essex in 1980 and were made up of Dave Gahan on vocals and Vince Clarke, Martin Gore and Andy Fletcher on keyboards. You can't really get more new wave than a band that deliberately placed style over substance and eschewed the use of any acoustic guitars or drums, preferring drum machines and synthesisers. Skinny, with crazy hair and a fashion style that blended flouncy shirts, leather, tartans and fetish gear, Depeche Mode were unashamedly pop and the perfect example of how chart music would develop in the early '80s. Their debut album, *Speak and Spell*, is the epitome of '80s new wave, a synth-pop cracker with hooks and melody to spare. Third single 'Just Can't Get Enough' became their first top 10 hit and one of the all-time classic synth-pop songs. Vince Clarke left after *Speak and Spell* to form Yazoo with Alison Moyet and then Erasure with Andy Bell, but not before he could put his historical stamp on the evolution of synth pop. Martin Gore would take over writing duties, and Alan Wilder joined the band. Second album *A Broken Frame* contained jaunty synth-pop love songs ('See You', 'Photograph of You') and moodier, more sensitive pieces ('My Secret Garden' and 'The Sun & the Rainfall'). Depeche Mode would become a darker band, evolving alongside the synthesiser. The lyrics started to show more depth, and dealt with both personal and larger themes like politics and the environment. *Some Great Reward* (1984) featured a pivotal song, 'Blasphemous Rumours', which set a new direction for the band. After this record they would release three hit albums in a row – *Black Celebration* (1986), *Music for the Masses* (1987) and *Violator* (1990). *Songs of Faith and Devotion* (1993) and *Ultra* (1997) would help them do what many UK new wave bands struggled to do – conquer America.

Dave Vince Martin & Andy

The band personally delivered their demo tape to record companies but met with resistance. Dave Gahan said, 'Most of them would tell us to fuck off. They'd say "leave the tape with us" and we'd say "it's our only one".'

In 1977, Vince Clarke and Andy Fletcher were playing in a band they had formed at school called No Romance In China. In '79, Clarke was the guitarist in The Plan, influenced by John Foxx—era Ultravox. Gore was in an acoustic duo called Norman and the Worms. In '79 Gore formed a band with friends called French Look. By 1980, Gore, Fletcher and Clarke had formed a band called Composition of Sound.

In the mid '90s Alan Wilder quit the band, saying he felt undervalued. Dave Gahan had his own problems. Addicted to heroin and cocaine, he missed recording sessions and only sporadically recorded vocals. After an overdose resulting in a near-death experience, Gahan entered rehab, cleaned up and the band released *Ultra*.

Budgie and Siouxsie were in a long-
term relationship; they married in
1991 and moved to France in 1996,
but divorced in 2007.

Siouxsie & The Banshees

Siouxsie suggested that she and Severin play when
a band pulled out of a 100 Club slot slated for
20 September 1976. They had no band name and
no other members so they recruited Marco Pirroni
(who played with Adam Ant) on guitar and Sid Vicious
on drums. A warped, off-the-cuff version of 'The
Lord's Prayer' filled their 20 minute set.

Formed in 1976 in London by Siouxsie Sioux (Susan Ballion) and Steve Severin (Steven Bailey), with John McKay joining as guitarist and Kenny Morris as drummer, Siouxsie and the Banshees mixed punk rock with warped playground chants, folk horror and twisted nursery rhymes. Visually, the band favoured a muted colour palette (the Banshees rocked various shades of black) but sonically they dealt in bright, abrasive guitar sounds and strident vocals, with Siouxsie the ringleader of a dark and damaged carnival. Part of the so-called Bromley Contingent, Siouxsie was already a known figure in the punk scene, but her foray into the music world would take punk into newer, more expansive territory. Debut single 'Hong Kong Garden' was an instant hit. Punk would never have used a xylophone in a song, let along as the introduction, but it would have employed the abrasive guitars and cocky stance of the Banshees. Debut album *The Scream* followed in 1978, a true foreshadowing of the post-punk sound, prompting NME journalist Nick Kent to write, 'Certainly, the traditional three-piece sound has never been used in a more unorthodox fashion with such stunning results.'

In 1980, Siouxsie and the Banshees
played secret gigs under the name
Janet and the Icebergs. One was a dual
gig with Altered Images at Brady's in
Liverpool on 9 September 1980.

In 1983 Siouxsie formed alternative supergroup
The Glove with Robert Smith (The Cure) and
Steve Severin. They released one album, *Blue
Sunshine*. Siouxsie and Budgie also formed their
own Banshees spin-off band The Creatures, who
released four albums: *Feast* (1983), *Boomerang*
(1989), *Anima Animus* (1999) and *Hai!* (2003).

Join Hands (1979) continued the Banshees' shaping of future sounds, planting the seeds of Goth, indie pop and industrial music. By the time the band released *Kaleidoscope* in 1980 and *Juju* in 1981, McKay had been replaced by John McGeoch, while The Cure's Robert Smith, who clearly had an affiliation with the Banshees, filled in on live guitar duties. Budgie (Peter Clarke) became permanent drummer. McGeoch shaped the Banshees' sound further and they expanded into psychedelia, Eastern music influences and unexpected instrumentation. The band released 11 studio albums and 30 singles, including two that made the top 10 ('Hong Kong Garden' and 'Dear Prudence') on the UK charts. Among those influenced by the Banshees are Suede, LCD Soundsystem (who covered 'Slowdive'), Slowdive (who named themselves after the same song), My Bloody Valentine, Garbage, Tricky, Air, Smashing Pumpkins, The Jesus and Mary Chain, Bloc Party and Sonic Youth.

Siouxsie Steve John & Kenny

Famous for her 'cat eye' make-up, Siouxsie has an obsession with felines and owned three cats – Spooky, Spider and Dandy.

Guitarist John McGeoch died in 2004. He is often cited as one of the most influential guitarists of all time and was greatly admired by Johnny Marr (The Smiths), Jonny Greenwood (Radiohead), John Frusciante (Red Hot Chili Peppers) and Dave Navarro (Jane's Addiction), among others. Artists who employed his guitar skills include Magazine, Visage, Generation X, Peter Murphy and Public Image Ltd.

Gary Numan has a pilot's licence and attempted to fly around the world in 1981 (and succeeded in 1982) to play a series of very premature farewell concerts. He was arrested in India on suspicion of spying and smuggling.

Gary Numan/ Tubeway Army

On Tubeway Army's first release, 'That's Too Bad', Gary Numan was listed under the name 'Valerian'.

Drummer Jess Lidyard said, 'He [Gary] told me he was going to have this hit with a song called 'Cars', and this was years before he'd actually written the music. When 'Are "Friends" Electric?' became a big success, he said that the order had gone wrong and it wasn't supposed to happen that way.'

UK whimsical comedy show *The Mighty Boosh* had a fond affection for Gary Numan, who was mentioned in several episodes and even appeared in one, 'The Power of the Crimp', in which he is shut in a cupboard. In the episode 'In Tundra', Noel enlists Numan to fly them to the Arctic tundra in his private jet (an animation shows them flying in the jet to the soundtrack of 'Cars'). He later asks a polar bear if he likes Gary Numan. In 'Hitcher', Noel's car mixtape consists of a stack of cassettes, all Gary Numan.

Gary Jess & Paul

Allegedly, Gary Numan chose
his new surname from the
Yellow Pages. He anglicised
the name of a plumber,
Arthur Neumann.

Gary Numan (Gary Webb) first came onto the music scene with the band Tubeway Army in 1977. The line-up consisted of Numan on vocals and guitars, Jess Lidyard on drums and Paul Gardiner on bass. Numan had played in two bands, Mean Street and The Lasers; he had met Gardiner in the latter. Tubeway Army released two albums – the eponymous, punk-meets-sci-fi debut and the follow-up chart hit, *Replicas*, which used fewer guitars and more synthesisers and ramped up the sci-fi overtones. Tubeway Army were one of the few bands to bridge the gap between punk and electronic music, taking their cues from John Foxx and Ultravox, Eno and David Bowie's *Low*, and the Nicholas Roeg–directed Bowie vehicle *The Man Who Fell to Earth*. The debut album's brittle guitars, angst-ridden vocals and dystopian allusions were new, and still sound distinctly like the 'birth of something'. By the time *Replicas* came along, the sound was still robotic and distant and the themes resolutely rooted in science-fiction stories and futuristic techno fear, but the sound had become warmer, more organic. Numan said, 'I was just a guitarist that played keyboards … I just turned punk songs into electronic songs.' Numan would drop the name Tubeway Army, make the band his back-up, and continue to release output under his name. *The Pleasure Principle* (1979), *Telekon* (1980) and *Dance* (1981) continued to expand and sculpt electronic sound, and would inform the electronic music of the future. Despite being popular during his career, and having several major chart hits, including 'Are "Friends" Electric?' and 'Cars', Numan would be derided by critics and the press and would find himself consigned to cult status. It must have been heartening, then, when later in life Numan was hailed as a pioneer of industrial, Gothic, rave and electronic music by bands and critics. The likes of Saint Etienne, Ladytron, Elastica, Basement Jaxx, Foo Fighters, Little Boots, Trent Reznor and Marilyn Manson all cite him as an influence.

Honourable mentions.

ECHO & THE BUNNYMEN
✖ **FORMED IN LIVERPOOL** in 1978, Echo & the Bunnymen were a four piece made up of Ian McCulloch on vocals, Will Sergeant on guitar, Les Pattinson on bass and Pete de Freitas on drums. Brittle, with soaring, chiming guitars and a lead singer who was rake thin, deathly pale and with a fountain of spiky black hair, Echo & the Bunnymen dealt in an anthemic, heroic brand of post-punk that heralded a new era of alternative bands. The Bunnymen had hit singles with 'The Cutter', 'The Killing Moon' and 'Bring On the Dancing Horses'. Classic albums include *Porcupine* and *Ocean Rain*. Pete de Freitas was killed in a motorcycle accident in 1989.

THE CARS
✖ **THE CARS** formed in Boston in 1976. The core of the band was Ric Ocasek on vocals and rhythm guitar, Benjamin Orr on vocals and bass, Elliot Eastern on lead guitar, Greg Hawkes on keyboards and David Robinson on drums. The Cars drew on a wide range of influences – minimal punk, pop, art rock and electronica – to form a unique new wave sound. The Cars sold over 20 million records and released several chart-topping singles including 'Drive', 'Shake It Up' and 'Let's Go'. Ocasek went on to establish a successful solo career. Orr died from pancreatic cancer in 2000 and Ocasek from cardiovascular disease in 2019.

TALK TALK
✖ **FORMING IN LONDON** in 1981, Talk Talk's line-up consisted of Mark Hollis on vocals, Paul Webb on bass, Simon Brenner on keyboards and Lee Harris on drums. While record companies tried to lump the band in with the New Romantic and synth-pop movements, Talk Talk wanted to forge their own path. Hollis' angst-ridden, sneering vocals and melancholy lyrics gave the band a depth that many synth-pop chart bands simply couldn't muster. The debut self-titled album was a minor hit, but follow up, *It's My Life*, was a major success and produced a top 10 hit with the title track, which was later covered by No Doubt. Talk Talk expanded their sound palette from there, releasing two sublime, ambient and atmospheric albums which featured experimental uses of time signatures, jazz progressions, space and silence. *The Colour of Spring* and *Spirit of Eden* are considered widely influential today. Hollis died in 2019 at the age of sixty-four.

NEW ORDER
✖ **AFTER THE DEATH** of Ian Curtis in 1980, the remaining members of Joy Division decided to carry on, albeit under a different name and with a new musical direction. Guitarist Bernard Sumner took over vocal duties, and keyboardist Gillian Gilbert joined bassist Peter Hook and drummer Stephen Morris later that year. →

NEW ORDER CONTINUED

→ New Order had experimented with keyboards on Joy Division tracks like 'Isolation', but they relied mainly on guitars. New Order blended the two instruments and later began to move towards more heavily synthesised sounds. Their classic track 'Blue Monday', released in 1983, remains the biggest selling 12" single of all time.

XTC

✖ XTC GOT TOGETHER in Swindon, England in 1972. The band were led by Andy Partridge on vocals and guitar and Colin Moulding on vocals and bass; the two were the principal songwriters. They were joined by Terry Chambers on drums and keyboardist Barry Andrews. With influences as diverse as punk, ska, dub, pop and experimental music, XTC forged a new style and sound. Quirky, angular and adventurous, XTC took post-punk and new wave to new realms. The band's skittish delivery and Partridge's mocking mannerisms both pilfered from, and pilloried, the excesses of punk rock. Early single 'Making Plans for Nigel' is credited with pioneering the '80s booming drum sound. While having several chart hits with tracks like 'Senses Working Overtime' and 'The Mayor of Simpleton', XTC still remained a cult band. Their album *Skylarking* was produced by Todd Rundgren and the diverse and impressive album *English Settlement* remains a benchmark of the new wave genre.

THE HUMAN LEAGUE

✖ DESPITE LATER mega-stardom, The Human League began life as a dark and highly experimental electronic outfit in Sheffield in 1977. As punk rock took over the nation, Martyn Ware and Ian Craig Marsh formed a band, The Futures. They were later joined by an untrained proto-pop star, Phil Oakey, on vocals, who had been known around the clubs for his avant-garde style of dress. Taking a new name from a 1974 board game, The Human League set about releasing robotic, sparse, doom-laden synthesiser punk over two LPs: *Reproduction* (1979) and *Travelogue* (1980) that featured proto–electro punk tracks like 'Being Boiled' and 'Empire State Human'. The band fought and manager Bob Last, in an effort to keep them all in his stable, suggested two bands. Oakey kept the name The Human League (and the band's debts) and recruited Susanne Sulley and Joanne Catherall, two schoolgirls he had spotted on the dancefloor at Crazy Daisy nightclub. Jo Callis joined on guitars, Ian Burden on keyboards and bass, and Philip Adrian Wright, who had been in the earlier version of The Human League, also came on board. They went on to have huge success with the album *Dare*, while Ware and Marsh would also find fame, along with vocalist Glenn Gregory, in Heaven 17. Between them they influenced generations of synth pop, experimental electronica, techno, rave, Goth, industrial and '80s chart.

THE PSYCHEDELIC FURS

✖ BEGINNING LIFE IN LONDON in 1977, The Psychedelic Furs are made up of Richard Butler on vocals and his brother Tim on guitar. The pivotal post-punk line-up also added Vince Ely on drums, John Ashton on guitar and Duncan Kilburn on saxophone. Taking their cues from punk, The Furs forged a dark, abrasive sound bed that lay under poetic, politically and socially charged lyrics. Richard Butler's raspy, bitter vocals towered over the sound, giving it a jubilant defiance. The addition of a saxophone was also a smart move for a band hovering at the tail end of punk, helping to set up a softer and more accessible future sound. John Hughes used 'Pretty in Pink' from their wonderful second album *Talk Talk Talk* (1981) as the title for his 1986 film. The Furs track was remixed for the soundtrack (which also featured other new wave stalwarts like OMD and New Order), providing a much smoother, chart-friendly version of what was originally a twisted tale of sex and intrigue complemented by cut-up lyrics and swirling rock guitars. The Furs would have several hit singles in the '80s, including 'Heaven', 'Love My Way' and 'The Ghost in You'.

ALSO LISTEN TO:

✖ The Pop Group, Pere Ubu, The Residents, The Fall, Adam and the Ants, Orange Juice, Buggles, Simple Minds, The B-52s, The Teardrop Explodes, The Jam, Blancmange, ABC, China Crisis, Yazoo, Thompson Twins, The Vapors, Soft Cell, Bow Wow Wow, The Fixx, Thomas Dolby, Tears for Fears, The Pretenders, Fad Gadget.

NEW WAVE 'ONE-HIT WONDERS'

· Plastic Bertrand, 'Ca Plane Pour Moi'
· Kajagoogoo, 'Too Shy'
· Nena, '99 Red Balloons'
· Men Without Hats, 'Safety Dance'
· Fiction Factory, 'Feels Like Heaven'
· A Flock Of Seagulls, 'I Ran'
· Modern English, 'I Melt With You'
· Bow Wow Wow, 'I Want Candy'
· The Vapors, 'Turning Japanese'
· Buggles, 'Video Killed the Radio Star'
· Wall of Voodoo, 'Mexican Radio'
· 'Til Tuesday, 'Voices Carry'
· Peter Schilling, 'Major Tom'

INDUSTRIAL AND ELECTRONICA

· Cabaret Voltaire
· Fad Gadget
· SPK
· The Normal
· Throbbing Gristle

2 TONE

· Madness
· The Specials
· The Selecter
· The Beat
· Bad Manners

PARALLEL SCENES

NEW ROMANTIC

· Ultravox
· Duran Duran
· Spandau Ballet
· Visage
· Seona Dancing
· Classix Nouveaux

MOD REVIVAL

· The Jam
· The Style Council
· Nine Below Zero
· Secret Affair
· The Lambrettas
· Purple Hearts
· The Merton Parkas

The look. The lifestyle.

Both post-punk and new wave had definite **'uniforms'** demonstrating allegiance to the cause. If you were into the new wave scene you had to look the part. The styles were subtler than in punk – in some cases you could even get away with your look at the office or your factory job, although you would probably have to tone down the hair. **Piercings** could be a problem, too, but they could be removed, leaving a look consisting of actual suits, pants, good shoes and crisp shirts. With some slight adjustments you could not only look acceptable, but presentable – even well put together. Nighttime was when you'd come alive, dressing to the hilt for clubbing, or dressing in **dark clothes** with **gelled hair** for a live gig. For the New Romantics, it was over-the-top costumes with a blend of the historical, the European and the fanciful, with make-up on women and men alike and the subversion of gender norms. Post-punk fans tended to dress down and dark, but still went heavy on the ozone-depleting hairspray to create stiffened fountains of hair and sight-robbing fringes. Shades were worn both night and day.

As the world moved out of the struggling '70s into a more affluent decade, work (and therefore money) was more readily available. So was information, through style magazines like *The Face* and *i-D* and the boom in youth-based music and lifestyle television shows. Alternative clubbing emerged, and meant that you could hear the latest music and get the latest looks. A plethora of smaller live venues and polytechnic college campuses hosted the likes of Joy Division and Gang of Four and bred a group of dead earnest, morose, passionate and existentially minded types. Various New Romantic nightclubs (such as Steve Strange and Rusty Egan's Blitz and Club For Heroes) gave night owls licence to live out their fashion fantasies, and the looks often spilled out into the fashion of the everyday. Technology played its part as well. Just as machines were reshaping music, they were also influencing fashion. Robotic dancing, jackets with clean lines, military uniforms and jumpsuits in techno fabrics, android-like dark glasses, and mathematical shapes in bright colours all gave new wave style a futuristic gleam. Philip K. Dick's novel *Do Androids Dream of Electric Sheep?* was made into the film *Blade Runner* (1982), and the fashion of replicant characters Roy Batty and Pris Stratton was echoed in the nightclub dress of the time. In 1984, William Gibson wrote *Neuromancer*, kicking off the technology age and sending terms like 'hacking' and 'cyberspace' into the everyday vernacular. Power suits, shoulder pads and absurdly gaudy geometrical earrings were just around the corner.

POST-PUNK FASHION

· Western neckerchiefs
· Mohair jumpers
· Gelled spiky hair
· Blazer covered in band badges
· Obscure indie band T-shirts
· Badge and shoelace neckties
· Combat boots, Dr. Martens, thrift-store shoes
· Military clothing
· Studded belts
· Overcoats
· Body shirts
· Shades
· Pearls

NEW WAVE FASHION

· Leather jackets
· Leather pants
· Pleated pants
· Skinny ties
· Pointy shoes
· Fountain of dyed hair with a floppy or spiky fringe
· Bright colours
· Leather skirts
· Geometric patterns
· Ironic military jackets
· Tutus
· Oversized neckerchiefs
· Cummerbunds
· Oversized sunglasses
· Thin belts

BEST NEW WAVE HAIRCUTS

· A Flock of Seagulls
· Adam Ant
· Limahl
· Sigue Sigue Sputnik
· Vince Clarke (Depeche Mode)

HOW TO BE A POST-PUNK BAND

NAME: Connotations of bleakness and starkness, short, open to interpretation.

KEYBOARD: Used to create 'texture', not as a main instrument.

GUITAR: Effects laden, brittle, chiming, jangly, manipulated – the lead line is king.

VOCALS: Grip the mic and stare intensely at the audience. Overly serious and sincere lyric delivery. Mostly stand still but with occasional bursts of feverish activity and outbreaks of uncontrolled dancing.

DRUMS: Booming, cavernous, minimal fills, sparse arrangements.

AUDIENCE: Swaying passionately while clutching a beer. Occasional nods of approval. Eyes closed in deep focus. Glancing around the room to sneer at other looks. Hiding under fringe. Trying not to smile.

HOW TO BE A NEW WAVE BAND

NAME: As long and pretentious as possible, something like Moonlight Waveform Organisation.

KEYBOARD: Stand behind the keyboard, expressionless and motionless. Using more than one finger to play is frowned upon. You could use two fingers at a stretch, but not from the same hand. Never make eye contact with the camera or the audience.

GUITAR: So dated.

VOCALS: Floaty and buried in the mix.

DRUMS: Should either be a drum machine, or electronic drums played along to a drum machine. Sparse, clipped and electronic.

AUDIENCE: Swaying dispassionately. Glancing around the room to compare and 'be inspired by' looks. Admiring and discussing the band's keyboards and synth drums, or ruminating on whether the 'keytar' (keyboard–guitar hybrid) is acceptable or not.

Influences & influencers.

Post-punk and new wave both came at a time of musical freedom and experimentation, which had developed out of the punk DIY ethos. It was a time of sudden and striking changes in fashion and technology, both of which fed into the genres' sounds and styles. Images of Joy Division, The Cure or the Bunnymen glaring gloomily at the camera in stark black and white, contrasted with colourful tableaux of synth bands with space-age clothes and gravity-defying hair cavorting behind streamlined keyboards, or rake-thin guitar bands with floppy hair, are a record of the times. But existing independently or in tandem with these acts were earlier bands or artists that had anticipated and influenced the sounds, people who documented the post-punk and new wave period, champions of the sounds and the bands, movers and shakers within the scene, and certain figures who would forever be associated with it.

JULIAN COPE

✖ AS FRONT MAN FOR The Teardrop Explodes and a leading figure in the Liverpool music scene, Cope had much to contribute to the development of post-punk and new wave pop. However, it would be his reviews and music writing that would prove to have an immediate impact on the formation of the genres. Cope's championing of the hermetic Scott Walker (he curated compilation LP *Fire Escape In The Sky: The Godlike Genius of Scott Walker*), and his obsessive written commentaries on the works of Syd Barrett greatly shaped the emerging post-punk and new wave scene, and a little later the Scottish underground and shoegaze movements.

ANTON CORBIJN

✖ DUTCH PHOTOGRAPHER Anton Corbijn was in his early twenties when he snapped some of the most iconic images of Joy Division, including the subterranean silhouettes of the band at Lancaster Gate tube station in London. Corbijn would also work with other new wave artists, including Depeche Mode, Kim Wilde, Elvis Costello, Siouxsie and the Banshees, Morrissey and Simple Minds.

IAN CURTIS

✖ AS FRONTMAN FOR JOY DIVISION, Ian Curtis embodies the post-punk spirit. Tortured and introspective, Curtis would spawn a legion of clones – skulking, sallow youths in long coats, smoking and wandering the streets, casting dark existential poetry toward the clouds, angst-ridden, forever searching ... or was that just me?

DELIA DERBYSHIRE

✖ DELIA DERBYSHIRE was a pioneer in the field of electronic music. Working with the BBC in the '60s, she used found sounds and synthesisers to build an impressive body of work that took in soundtracks, incidental sounds and experimental electronic music. Her reworking of Ron Grainer's orchestral *Doctor Who* theme was a pivotal influence on the new wave movement.

HOWARD DEVOTO

✖ AS PART OF THE BUZZCOCKS, Howard Devoto was essential to the development of punk rock, the DIY music movement and independent labels. Not content with those achievements, Devoto also became one of the progenitors of post-punk with his band Magazine. Their early albums – *Real Life* in 1978 and *Secondhand Daylight* in 1979 – were the templates for the British post-punk sound, while many new wave artists owe a debt to 1980's slicker and more electronic *The Correct Use of Soap* and the single 'A Song From Under the Floorboards'.

TOP SIX MOST PRETENTIOUS NEW WAVE BAND NAMES

· Orchestral Manoeuvres in the Dark
· Echo & the Bunnymen
· A Flock Of Seagulls
· The British Electric Foundation
· Cabaret Voltaire
· Depeche Mode

BRIAN ENO/ DAVID BOWIE

✖ BRIAN ENO had begun his experimentation with electronic music while in Roxy Music. The replacement of the lead break with a synth break in their track 'Virginia Plain' was effectively the starting point for electronic music, new wave and techno – and it happened in 1972. Eno would pre-empt punk, post-punk, new wave and ambient music with a string of albums during the early and mid '70s. In particular, *Here Come the Warm Jets*, *Taking Tiger Mountain (By Strategy)* and *Another Green World* explored loose pop, the marriage of guitar and synthesiser, noise, ambience and brittle, melancholic pop. David Bowie's album *Low*, produced by Eno, was a major turning point in synthesiser-based rock: its short, incisive, dark guitar pop and experimental, ambient instrumentals are rightfully hailed as key influences on post-punk and new wave. Bowie's 'Ashes to Ashes' was a snapshot of the sound – a perfect encapsulation of the themes and styles at the centre of post-punk and new wave – and heralded the commercial potential of synthesiser music.

TREVOR HORN

✖ **WELL KNOWN FOR** his production work with Frankie Goes To Hollywood, Yes, the Pet Shop Boys, Propaganda and The Art of Noise, as well as the creation of the ZTT record label, Trevor Horn was also the brain behind the Buggles, who became a major influence on future synth pop and new wave. *The Age of Plastic* (1980) and single 'Video Killed the Radio Star' blended synthesiser, guitars and vocal effects to create a blueprint for how early '80s new wave pop would sound.

KRAFTWERK

✖ **GERMAN ELECTRONIC PIONEERS** Kraftwerk began making cinematic popular music with the synthesiser as far back as 1969. Their albums *Autobahn* (1974), *Radio-Activity* (1975), *Trans-Europe Express* (1977) and *The Man-Machine* (1978), which includes hit single 'The Model', were highly influential on '80s synth-pop musicians and remain a touchstone for electronic musicians today.

MARK E. SMITH

✖ **AS MARK E. SMITH SAID,** 'If it's me and yer granny on bongos, it's The Fall', highlighting the all-encompassing originality of one of post-punk's greatest mavericks. With an extraordinary output, a legion of devoted followers and a laconic, self-deprecating vocal delivery, Mark E. Smith, with The Fall, accentuated the fact that post-punk was all about self-expression, the exploration of human frailties and quirks, and if you felt like it, a fine range of slacks and knitwear.

ROBERT SMITH

✖ **AS LEAD SINGER OF THE CURE,** Smith helped to shape the music of the post-punk era – but not only that. Smith's iconic looks, from the early crop-haired punk outsider in black to the tangle-haired, make-up smeared, oversized-jumper-wearing proto-Goth teddy bear, are some of the most enduring images in the post-punk visual canon.

STEVE STRANGE

✖ STEPHEN HARRINGTON, otherwise known as Steve Strange, was a flamboyant nightclub promoter and musician. After seeing the Sex Pistols in his home town in Wales, he moved to London and began working for Malcolm McLaren. In 1978 he formed Visage, a proto–new wave band that released a debut self-titled album in 1980 that spawned the hit 'Fade to Grey'. Strange was host at the Blitz club in Covent Garden, where new wave found a home. Stylish or outrageous costumes were essential and many of the fashions there, and the people who frequented the club, informed the New Romantic movement.

ROBERT MOOG/ PETER VOGEL

✖ ROBERT MOOG DEBUTED the first commercial synthesiser in 1964. The Moog synthesiser, and a more portable model released in 1971, were pivotal to the burgeoning post-punk/new wave scenes. Associated concepts like pitch control, frequencies and modularity are still intrinsic to electronic music today. Peter Vogel took it a step further with the Fairlight CMI (short for Computer Musical Instrument) in 1979. An early 'music workstation', it could record sounds and they could then be played on a keyboard. Sampling, as it became known, is the bedrock for much electronic music to this day.

TOP POST-PUNK RECORD LABELS

- Factory
- Rough Trade
- Attrix
- Sire
- Good Vibrations
- Beggars Banquet
- 4AD
- Ace of Hearts
- Fast Product
- New Hormones
- Hot Records
- Situation Two (Beggars Banquet offshoot)
- Postcard Records
- 53rd & 3rd

TOP FIVE POST-PUNK & NEW WAVE VENUES

- Blitz
- Heaven
- Mud Club
- The Fridge
- Billy's

The legacy.

Despite being an alienating, abrasive and self-centred genre, punk was genial enough to open many doors and usher in whoever cared to step inside. Once the Sex Pistols had topped the charts, two things happened. Anyone with a leaning towards the musically creative thought, 'Hey, I can do that', and record companies thought, 'Hey, we can market that'. Indie labels exploded; bands that sounded a bit off but had a special something were snapped up in droves. The upshot was a flourishing of creativity that fans of experimental, underground or emotive music could only dream of. All of a sudden, artists like The Cure, Siouxsie and the Banshees and Gary Numan were not only making music, but also topping the charts. *Top of the Pops* and *Countdown* would play an Elton John track followed by a sparse, doom-laden Cure or Echo & the Bunnymen single without batting an eyelid. Morrissey would flounce about onstage in between performances by Dr. Hook and Cliff Richard. Art Garfunkel's 'Bright Eyes' would be replaced in the number one chart position by

Tubeway Army's 'Are "Friends" Electric?'; Ian Dury & the Blockheads' 'Hit Me With Your Rhythm Stick' would be number one one week and 'Y.M.C.A.' by the Village People would be number one the next. Among it all would be a kind of new wave commercial hybrid – bands who used the new sound but had myriad hits, like The Boomtown Rats, The Police, The Pretenders or Blondie. It's not hard to see how music changed after post-punk and new wave had further shaped the ideas of punk. Pop in the '80s became more outrageous. Hip-hop emerged from the shadows and displayed a true punk ethos. Bedroom producers started to make sample-heavy dance music. House music flourished, as did acid house, techno and rave after that – all were imbued with the spirit of post-punk and new wave experimentalism. In the early 2000s, artists began to directly refer to the post-punk and new wave bands of the past. To this day, the rebellious and restless spirit of that age continues to appeal to and inspire musicians, and to shape new music.

✖ GOTH/ETHERAL

The Cure and Siouxsie and the Banshees turned to a darker sound and style and pivoted into a genre that became known (to the bands' distaste) as Goth, or Gothic rock. Later movements like emo and cold wave would draw heavily from Goth.

Key artists: The Sisters of Mercy, Bauhaus, The Cult, Clan Of Xymox, Alien Sex Fiend, Gene Loves Jezebel, Dead Can Dance, Cocteau Twins, Strawberry Switchblade, The Mission, Killing Joke, The Damned, Fields Of The Nephilim.

✖ DANCE CROSSOVER

Indie tunes were made dancefloor ready with added grooves, funky rhythms and tasty beats.

Key artists: The Soup Dragons, The Beloved (second phase), That Petrol Emotion, Happy Mondays, Paris Angels.

✖ SHOEGAZE

Lo-fi recording, drone, spiritual and ethereal tones, effects pedal overload and experimentation saw psychedelia and indie blossom into shoegaze (also known as The Scene That Celebrates Itself and later, dream pop). My Bloody Valentine had formed and started putting out EPs in 1985. 1988's *You Made Me Realise* and 1990's *Glider* EP set the template for (and also defied) the classic shoegaze sound.

Key artists: My Bloody Valentine, Slowdive, Ride, Telescopes, Moose, Chapterhouse, Revolver.

✖ SCOTTISH UNDERGROUND

NME's C86 cassette, psychedelia and Americana combined to produce a brace of bands who defined the northern British independent sound. A lo-fi approach to recording and a DIY approach to making records grew out of punk, and in turn influenced the burgeoning grunge and slacker movements in the US.

Key artists: The Pastels, Teenage Fanclub, Primal Scream, The Vaselines, BMX Bandits, the Shop Assistants.

✖ INDIE POP, ANORAK JANGLE & SHAMBLING

Post-punk's chiming guitar lines and new wave's melodic sensibility gave rise to a wave of 'anorak' bands (the uniform of choice) who created short, sharp bursts of perfect pop running alongside the emergence of independent labels and an independent music chart.

Key artists: The Wedding Present, McCarthy, The Brilliant Corners, Mighty Mighty, The Bodines, The Chesterfields, The Flatmates, The Sundays, The Smiths, Lloyd Cole and the Commotions, Aztec Camera, The Beloved, The Corn Dollies.

✖ C86

NME's C86 cassette capitalised on an emerging scene and became a pivotal point between the post-punk and new wave movements and the indie music scene.

Key artists: Primal Scream, Stump, Mighty Mighty, The Bodines, The Mighty Lemon Drops, Close Lobsters, McCarthy, The Wedding Present, Half Man Half Biscuit, The Pastels.

✖ POST-PUNK & NEW WAVE LEGACY BANDS

Interpol, Bloc Party, Franz Ferdinand, The Strokes, Pulp, Maximo Park, LCD Soundsystem, The Futureheads, Elastica, The Killers, The Rapture, Yeah Yeah Yeahs, Kaiser Chiefs, Modest Mouse, Arcade Fire, Muse, Ash, Arctic Monkeys, Editors, The Church, Foals, Graham Coxon, The Kills, Suede, Underworld.

✖ POLITICAL POP

Thatcherism and unemployment in the UK left plenty to complain about, and the early to mid '80s was rife with bands making social and political statements in catchy pop tunes that snuck into the charts like Trojan horses. The post-Reagan era in America saw the rise of aggressive punk rock–inspired bands who railed against the system like Bad Religion, Crass and Minor Threat.

Key artists: The Style Council, Billy Bragg, The Beat, Gang of Four, The Housemartins, The Specials, Heaven 17, Elvis Costello.

Select disco-graphy.

Blondie

· Blondie (1976)
· Plastic Letters (1977)
· Parallel Lines (1978)
· Eat to the Beat (1979)
· Autoamerican (1980)

Cabaret Voltaire

· Mix-Up (1979)
· The Voice of America (1980)
· Red Mecca (1981)
· 2X45 (1982)
· The Crackdown (1983)
· Johnny Yesno (1983)
· Micro-Phonies (1984)

The Cars

· The Cars (1978)
· Candy-O (1979)
· Panorama (1980)
· Shake It Up (1981)

The Cure

· Three Imaginary Boys (1979)
· Seventeen Seconds (1980)
· Faith (1981)
· Pornography (1982)
· The Top (1984)
· The Head on the Door (1985)

Depeche Mode

· Speak & Spell (1981)
· A Broken Frame (1982)
· Construction Time Again (1983)
· Some Great Reward (1984)
· Black Celebration (1986)
· Music for the Masses (1987)
· Violator (1990)

Devo

· Q: Are We Not Men?
  A: We Are Devo! (1978)
· Duty Now for the Future (1979)
· Freedom of Choice (1980)

Echo & the Bunnymen

· Crocodiles (1980)
· Heaven Up Here (1981)
· Porcupine (1983)
· Ocean Rain (1984)

**Elvis Costello
& the Attractions**
· *Armed Forces* (1979)
· *Get Happy!!* (1980)

Gang of Four
· *Entertainment* (1979)
· *Solid Gold* (1981)
· *Songs of the Free* (1982)

The Human League
· *Reproduction* (1979)
· *Travelogue* (1980)
· *Dare* (1981)

Japan
· *Adolescent Sex* (1978)
· *Obscure Alternatives* (1978)
· *Quiet Life* (1979)
· *Gentleman Take Polaroids* (1980)
· *Tin Drum* (1981)

Joy Division
· *Unknown Pleasures* (1979)
· *Closer* (1980)

Magazine
· *Real Life* (1978)
· *Secondhand Daylight* (1979)
· *The Correct Use of Soap* (1980)

New Order
· *Movement* (1981)
· *Power, Corruption & Lies* (1983)
· *Low-life* (1985)

Orange Juice
· *You Can't Hide Your Love Forever* (1982)
· *Rip It Up* (1982)

Orchestral Manoeuvres in the Dark
· *Orchestral Manoeuvres in the Dark* (1980)
· *Organisation* (1980)
· *Architecture & Morality* (1981)
· *Dazzle Ships* (1983)
· *Junk Culture* (1984)

The Pop Group
· *Y* (1979)
· *For How Much Longer Do We Tolerate Mass Murder?* (1980)

The Psychedelic Furs
· *The Psychedelic Furs* (1980)
· *Talk Talk Talk* (1981)
· *Forever Now* (1982)

Siouxsie and the Banshees
· *The Scream* (1978)
· *Join Hands* (1979)
· *Kaleidoscope* (1980)

The Smiths
· *The Smiths* (1984)
· *Meat is Murder* (1985)
· *The Queen is Dead* (1986)
· *Strangeways, Here We Come* (1987)

Talking Heads
· *Talking Heads: 77* (1977)
· *More Songs About Buildings and Food* (1978)
· *Fear of Music* (1979)
· *Remain in Light* (1980)
· *Speaking in Tongues* (1983)

Talk Talk
· *The Party's Over* (1982)
· *It's My Life* (1984)
· *The Colour of Spring* (1986)
· *Spirit of Eden* (1988)

The Teardrop Explodes
· *Kilimanjaro* (1980)
· *Wilder* (1981)

Throbbing Gristle
· *The Second Annual Report* (1977)
· *D.o.A.: The Third and Final Report*
  of Throbbing Gristle (1978)
· *20 Jazz Funk Greats* (1979)

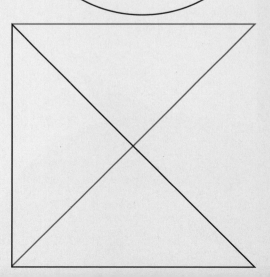

Tubeway Army / Gary Numan
· *Tubeway Army* (1978)
· *Replicas* (1979)
· *The Pleasure Principle* (1979)
  (as Gary Numan)
· *Telekon* (1980)
  (as Gary Numan)

Ultravox
· *Ultravox!* (1977) (with John Foxx)
· *Ha! Ha! Ha!* (1977) (with John Foxx)
· *Systems of Romance* (1978)
  (with John Foxx)
· *Vienna* (1980) (with Midge Ure)
· *Metamatic* (1980) (John Foxx solo)

Visage
· *Visage* (1980)
· *The Anvil* (1982)

Wire
· *Pink Flag* (1977)
· *Chairs Missing* (1978)
· *154* (1979)

XTC
· *Drums and Wires* (1979)
· *Black Sea* (1980)
· *English Settlement* (1982)

Smith Street Books

Published in 2020 by Smith Street Books
Naarm | Melbourne | Australia
smithstreetbooks.com

ISBN: 978-1-925811-76-6

Publisher: Paul McNally
Project manager: Lucy Heaver, Tusk Studio
Editor: Rowena Robertson
Designer: Michelle Mackintosh

Printed & bound in China by C&C Offset
Printing Co., Ltd.

Book 134
10 9 8 7 6 5 4 3 2 1

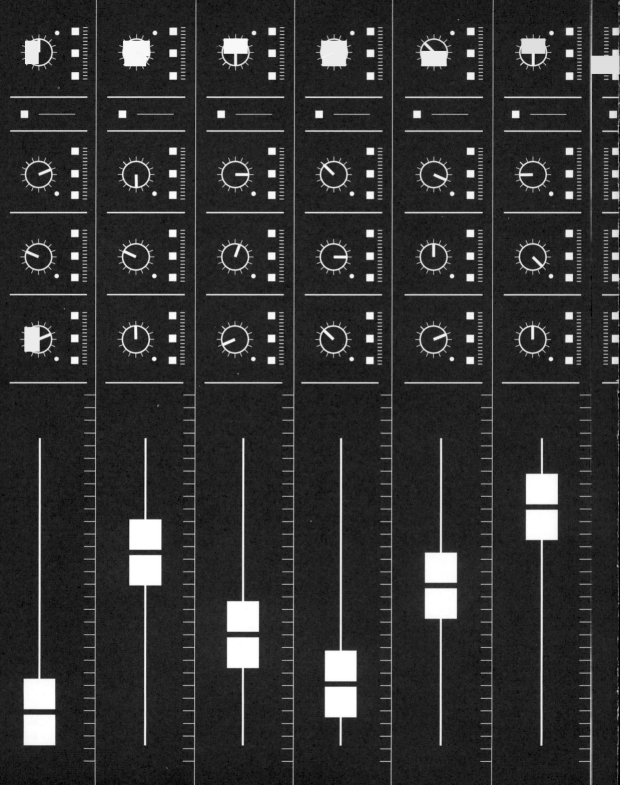